THE JOB SEARCH CHECKLIST

Everything You Need to Know
to Get Back to Work After a Layoff

DAMIAN BIRKEL

AMACOM

New York • Atlanta • Brussels • Chicago • Mexico City • San Francisco
Shanghai • Tokyo • Toronto • Washington, D.C.

Bulk discounts available. For details visit:
www.amacombooks.org/go/specialsales
Or contact special sales:
Phone: 800-250-5308
Email: specialsls@amanet.org
View all the AMACOM titles at: www.amacombooks.org
American Management Association: www.amanet.org

This publication is designed to provide accurate and authoritative information in regard to the subject matter covered. It is sold with the understanding that the publisher is not engaged in rendering legal, accounting, or other professional service. If legal advice or other expert assistance is required, the services of a competent professional person should be sought.

Library of Congress Cataloging-in-Publication Data

Birkel, Damian.
    The job search checklist : everything you need to know to get back to work after a layoff / Damian Birkel. — First Edition.
        pages cm
    Includes bibliographical references and index.
    ISBN-13: 978-0-8144-3291-4
    ISBN-10: 0-8144-3291-3
    1. Job hunting. 2. Résumés (Employment) 3. Career development. 4. Unemployed—Life skills guides. I. Title.
    HF5382.7.B557   2013
    650.14—dc23   2013012917

About AMA

American Management Association (www.amanet.org) is a world leader in talent development, advancing the skills of individuals to drive business success. Our mission is to support the goals of individuals and organizations through a complete range of products and services, including classroom and virtual seminars, webcasts, webinars, podcasts, conferences, corporate and government solutions, business books, and research. AMA's approach to improving performance combines experiential learning—learning through doing—with opportunities for ongoing professional growth at every step of one's career journey.

Printing number
10 9 8 7 6 5 4 3 2 1

CONTENTS

STEP 5 The Power of Networking

STEP 6 Effective Interviewing

Step 7 Reemployment: Hit the Ground Running

The samples and templates in the exhibits in this book can be accessed online and downloaded to your computer from: www.amacombooks.org/go/JobSearchChecklist

Job loss is the great equalizer. Regardless of your age, education, income, job level, or the company that you worked for, job loss changes your life. Without warning, you are plunged into a professional identity crisis, and thrown into a roiling sea of emotion.

The ones you love the most have also been affected by your abrupt unemployment. Like you, they have not had the chance to plan, prepare, or react. Everyday family routines are suddenly invaded and viewed through the lens of: *"Can we really afford this?"* Unemployment takes over emotionally, financially, socially, and psychologically: All because someone is out of work.

It is one thing to talk about how to manage job loss; it is another thing altogether to have lived through it and risen above it. That is why I was delighted when Damian asked me to write the Foreword to this book. I have watched him "practice what he preaches" while *he* was out of work, and I know well the power of *The Job Search Checklist* to get you through and beyond this extremely trying time.

Here you will find no theories. You will only find the proven, strategies that have worked for so many unemployed and under-employed people who have attended the Professionals in Transition® Support Group, Inc. (PIT®), both in person and online since 1992.

Finding a new job has nothing to do with luck. It has everything to do with how you think and the techniques you use to conduct your job search campaign. A talented young baseball player may be able to walk off the sandlots into a major league spring training camp, and occasionally connect with the ball. But to make it to the big leagues, he needs coaching in the finer points of the batter's trade. He needs to learn the techniques, and he must put them into practice. Many a player of mediocre talent has outshone more gifted performers by becoming a student of the game—and through sheer hustle.

The same goes for job searching. You can start your job search without coaching and without preparation, and occasionally you'll get an interview. But there's a wide chasm between scoring an occasional interview and actually landing a job. And the fastest way to find a job is to learn the proven real-world techniques offered in *The Job Search Checklist,* and *practice* them! Work hard as you practice, and then implement them. As you move ahead, stand tall, and be proud as you master each chapter of the book. Sometimes you'll be dealing with trial and error. But no matter what, continue to execute through the process. You won't be disappointed.

I believe that faithful courage and values-based living are essential cornerstones for both success and significance. What does this mean for you? Only you will know at the end of each day if you have put in the effort, and moved yourself closer to the prize of finding a job. But when you make your way through *The Job Search Checklist*, you will soon find that it's that glorious and sunny day that you hit the walk-off home run of your dreams into the golden field of your next dream job. With knowledge and practice, *it can happen.*

I wish you courage and all the best.

Dr. Nido Qubein
President, High Point University
Chairman, Great Harvest Bread Company

ACKNOWLEDGMENTS

No author *ever* writes a book alone. In fact, the process of writing a book reminds one of the Swahili proverb, "It takes a village to raise a child." This has been my experience with *The Job Search Checklist: Everything You Need to Know to Get Back to Work After a Layoff.* Its completion required a community of people, who brought their special talents to bear at just the right time, with the right expertise, and at the right place. This process enables all members of the village to meet the deadlines required to raise the child (or, in this case, the book) and keep things moving smoothly.

This book would not have been completed without the hundreds of hours invested by my Assistant, Linda Speaks. Her dedication, input, hard work, initiative, attention to detail, and willingness to go the extra mile has been phenomenal. "Thank you" cannot begin to encompass my gratitude for all of the outstanding work that she has done!

Special thanks to John Reidy and Candace Smith for translating my ideas into art. I cherish the time both of you took out of your busy schedules to create the diagrams that bring life to the concepts illustrated in this book. Your patience as we worked through issues was most appreciated. I am delighted that your illustrations will receive the national recognition that they deserve. My gratitude to Karyn Griffin, who believed in this project from its conception and helped me brainstorm the master diagram from which the entire book evolved.

I would also like to recognize journalist and Sergeant Arthur Mondale for discovering the link between Job Loss Grieving and Posttraumatic Stress Disorder (PTSD). My gratitude to professional photographer Dennis Kale, who took my picture for *The Job Search Checklist, Business Week Japan*, and for a *Wall Street Journal* cover story. Dennis has been a lifelong friend and always finds a way to bring out the best digital image in me.

Special thanks to Jeanie R. Ross, Director of Market Readiness and
Employment at Wake Forest University School of Business, and Charlotte
Center, Linda Groves, and Andréas Lino for their guidance and feedback
through the early stages of the project. I also appreciate the encouragement
provided by Chuck Chambers, Steve Nachman, Steve Guttenberg, Karen
Isgett, Judd and Carol Eseman, Myron Mitchell, Angela Mullins, Tim and
Jackie Dixon, Alan Krivoshey, Mark Shreck, Dennis O'Madigan, Fr. Brian
Cook, and Al Renna.

I would like to recognize the connectors in my life (those people in my
network who were responsible for helping me find the opportunity that ultimately became my next job), including Ed Buechel, Joe Greenfield, Dan
Comer, Bob Kieger, Barbara Talabisco, Beverly Bradstock, Melvin Scales,
and Dr. Ron Berra.

I am also delighted to acknowledge the contributions made by volun-
teers and board members (past and present) of Professionals In Transition®,
including Roger Pike, Chris McGee, Marcus Hamm, John Eiffe, Jack Degnon,
John Colthar, Dr. Bill Hartman, Don Witte, Bruce DeBole, Tom Desch, Bob
Merritt, Michael Kelly, Sherry Thrush, Glen Fortson, Chuck Hotchkiss,
David and Lisa Cox, J. R. Childress, Patt Shore, and Theresa Ehrens.

I would like to recognize Hank Kennedy, President and Publisher, and
the staff of AMACOM Books, particularly Ellen Kadin, Executive Editor;
William Helms 3rd, Associate Acquisitions Editor; Barry Richardson, Senior Development Editor; Andy Ambraziejus, Managing Editor; Jenny Wes-
selmann Schwartz, Director of Trade Sales and Marketing; Michael Sivilli,
Associate Editor; and Barbara A. Chernow and Carol Pierson of Chernow
Editorial Services, Inc.

Finally, it would not have been possible to write this book without the
love and support of my family. To my loving wife, Donna, for more than 35
years of marriage, patience, unwavering support, and belief in me, I thank
you daily, as the earth thanks the sun. Also, to my wonderful adult children,
Annie and John. Thank you, Lord, for the strength and faith that allowed
me to complete this work.

F inding a job is not easy—especially when you are unemployed. I've been out of work several times. I know all about having to struggle with the waves of emotion, the sleepless nights, the ongoing frustration, and the feelings of being worthless—cast aside like a piece of obsolete machinery. I, too, have had to live through the humiliation of having my professional identity stripped away and my income stream disrupted. I understand what it's like to cope with the rippling effect this crisis has on one's loved ones.

Right now, you may be experiencing what I went through during the times I was unemployed—you're in shock and suffering from information overload. You may be overwhelmed with job search materials, books, and internet sites; confused by conflicting expert opinions; and paralyzed by fear. During my job searches, I often thought, "Wouldn't it be great if there was some sort of master job search checklist to make sure everything was being done in the right order, at the right time, with the right résumé? Is there anything I am missing? What other materials do I need to make my job search a success?"

The Job Search Checklist will help you fill that gap. It will guide you through the step-by-step process of finding a job, while providing hope and validation. If you are looking for a battle plan developed and tested in the trenches of unemployment, you have found one. In this book, you will find:

- Key strategies built around a 7-Step Job Search Plan that will guide you through the reemployment process.
- Itemized checklists in each chapter detailing the action steps needed to successfully master critical issues, both emotional and practical, and to help build a complete job search plan of action.
- Proven, viable résumé formats, cover letters, networking letters of approach, and other job search correspondence.

- Access to templates, forms, and other examples of job search correspondence to help you customize your job search.

I Can Help You Find a Job

You are not alone. I have been in your shoes because I have lost my job *four times* throughout my career and have felt the shock, rage, humiliation, fogginess, depression, ongoing stress, and fear.

Over twenty years ago, I founded Professionals In Transition® Support Group Inc. (PIT®), a nationally and internationally recognized nonprofit, career support organization. (For more information on PIT®, see www .jobsearching.org). Our weekly support group meetings (run by volunteers) have been held every Thursday night at the American Red Cross center in Winston-Salem, North Carolina, since 1992. What is unique to PIT® is the recognition, by the worldwide media of our state-of-the-art job search techniques, as well as our emotional and practical support provided free of charge by our all-volunteer association. More than four thousand people have been touched by PIT® and thousands more have visited online.

In addition, I have reeducated myself and am now a nationally certified career counselor running an Employability Lab at our local community college. The road to reemployment is full of sharp curves, steep climbs, and sudden drops. This rough road is often unmarked and frequently marred by potholes of rejection. The so-called "information highway" known as the Internet has so many branches that getting lost, confronting a detour, hitting construction, reaching dead ends, or even falling into deep, dark, black holes are not only common, but can waste a huge chunk of your valuable time. It is my hope that *The Job Search Checklist* will help you navigate the road to reemployment and that by following the 7-Step Job Search Plan, you will create a roadmap to personal success.

How This Book Is Organized

The Job Search Checklist begins by addressing the extremely stressful "living-in-limbo" time period before a layoff or downsizing. This section provides indicators, strategies, and checklists to help you decode and react to the signs of an impending layoff, so that you can effectively prepare in advance regardless of whether you are affected.

From there, *The Job Search Checklist* is divided into seven steps, each of which is further divided into chapters. Throughout the chapters, you will find knowledge, advice, recommendations, templates, and checklists to guide your job search process.

The following explains what you can find in each step of the process (see Exhibit I-1).

Step 1: The Emotional Impact of Job Loss

Losing your job is one of the most traumatic things that will happen in your life. This section gives you a comprehensive understanding of your personal job loss grieving process, as well as how it will affect your family. This section will provide tools and tactics to manage both the personal and family tensions that arise, along with the waves of emotion that are created by job loss. In addition, the role of posttraumatic (delayed) and ongoing stress will be discussed and ways to avoid its paralyzing impact will be presented.

Step 2: Life After Unemployment

Recovery from job loss begins with small daily steps. Most people say that total recovery from the emotional impact of unemployment only happens over time. Critical matters need to be addressed in the first several weeks after unemployment begins, including the key things you need *to do* and *not do*, and why.

Another step in the recovery process is getting "job search" ready, including setting up a dedicated work space, establishing a daily routine, and understanding your game plan from this point forward. You will begin to gradually rebuild your professional identity. This process will take time because your spirit and desire are still quite fragile. You must accept your current situation and move forward to change what you can. The recovery process will help coordinate and align your thoughts before determining the next steps in your career.

Exhibit I-1 Job Search Steps

	Step 1: Emotional Impact of Job Loss	Step 2: Life After Unemployment	Step 3: Developing a Career Path	Step 4: Guidelines for Crafting an Effective Résumé	Step 5: The Power of Networking	Step 6: Interviewing & Salary Negotiation	Step 7: Hit the Ground Running
Chapters	1. Job Loss Grieving	3. Recovery	6. Developing a Plan	10. Résumé Components	15. The Visible Job Market (Advertised)	18. Informational Interviews	24. Your First 30 Days
	2. Secondhand Job Loss	4. Getting Organized	7. All-Important Research	11. Chronological or Functional (?)	16. In-Person Networking (Referrals)	19. Screening Interviews	25. 90 Days and Counting
		5. Rebuilding Your Professional Identity	8. Personality Testing	12. Keywords - The Language of the Internet	17. Social Networking (Online)	20. The Interview: Types and Styles	26. Conclusions
			9. Personal Marketing Plan	13. Challenging the Power of the Internet		21. The Interview: Concerns and Questions	
				14. Creating Internet-Friendly Documents		22. The Interview: Strategies to Ace an Interview	
						23. Salary Negotiation	

Step 3: Developing a Career Plan

No magic job fairy is suddenly going to appear on your doorstep, tap you on the head to make all the pain go away, and then miraculously cause a new job to appear. Instead, developing a career plan is a long and self-examining process. You begin with a series of exercises to help you pinpoint what you liked the most and least about your last job; help you determine your transferable skills; learn how to think outside of the box; and find out how to explore career fields.

A strong career plan is built on robust research. This section walks you through the many research options available to find key information about particular industries, companies, decision makers, and job openings. From there, personality testing and its role in the hiring process are discussed.

Creating a personal marketing plan is essential to promoting YOU. This includes developing critical segments like a Bridge Statement, Career Summary, 30-Second Commercial, Unique Differential Advantages, and much more.

Step 4: Crafting an Effective Résumé

A well-written résumé is crucial to your success and serves as your platform to market and promote YOU. This step discusses universal résumé segments that when combined create a clear, clean, and concise document. In addition, it will help you decide what type of résumé is best. You will learn about how to find job-associated keywords; the hidden language of the Internet; and the role of the applicant tracking system in determining whether your résumé gets read. Are you able to navigate the Internet; create Internet friendly documents; or enhance your résumé so that you are assured it gets read? These topics are discussed in Step 4.

Step 5: The Power of Networking

The single most important life skill you can teach yourself when job searching, both now and in the future, is in-person networking. Although 80 percent of all jobs are found through people, not the Internet, a recent study showed that only 4 percent of job search time is spent conducting in-person networking. Step 5 begins by giving you a proven, practical course in how to start in-person networking, its protocols and correspondence, and how to use that approach in your career as well as in your personal life.

Many other channels, such as social networking (also known as social media), have their own important part to play. You will be introduced to five important types of media sites. By concentrating on the most effective ones, you will be able to quickly learn, efficiently use, and successfully manage social media to help create a job search umbrella for you.

Step 6: Effective Interviewing

Successful interviewing will land you your next job. Interviewing is stressful, but it is a life skill. Types and styles of interviews (including informational, screening, and technical), along with concerns and questions, are provided to help you prepare. Finally, the dreaded subject but skillful art of how and when to effectively negotiate salary is discussed in detail.

Step 7: Hit the Ground Running

This final step is a celebration of your successful reentry into the job market. Key challenges and opportunities that you will face in the first few weeks and months of your new job are highlighted. Suggestions are made about how to manage the first six months, but like everything else, it is important to take a day at a time. You and your new professional image are working together to get back to normal—enjoy the fruits of your hard work.

Using the Checklists

Checklists are the backbone of this book. A checklist precedes each of the seven steps and another checklist appears at the end of each chapter. The step checklists highlight critical points of information detailed in greater depth in the individual chapters. You can skim the checklist to see if that step's information is relevant to you or if you should go on to the next job search step for topics that benefit you.

The checklist at the end of each chapter allows you to measure your progress every step of the way. The checklists provide the simple framework to start making sense of the enormous amount of information available relative to finding a job. The checklists help you to:

- Translate the business jargon of employers and human resource personnel.
- Understand the technological methods of filling available positions.
- Handle the realities of knowing what to do and how to organize yourself allowing you to break through the technical barrier of finding your next job.

The purpose of this book and the 7-Step Job Search Plan checklists is to give you the tools to rebound as quickly as possible in finding a "best-fit" means of gainful employment and getting your life back to normal. Your job now is finding a job, and this book provides the checklists, tools, and confidence to help you do just that.

PREQUELS: ANTICIPATING JOB LOSS

Before Losing Your Job

Get yourself organized, especially if rumors of layoffs are in the air or actual layoffs are already occurring. *Plan ahead!*

Monitor Changes in Your Workplace and Work Organization

Be aware of changes in management's behavior that might indicate change is coming. For example:

- Your boss won't look you in the eye.
- Management behaves evasively and avoids dealing with you directly.
- All HR and high-administrative personnel receive privacy screens for their computer monitors. They become defensive when approached, which is suspicious because they were always helpful and friendly.
- Administrative assistants who report to the director level or higher management give you "empathy" ("sad eyes") or guilt signs before anything has happened. If you are wondering why, it is probably because they have completed the latest organization chart and know that your name is not on it.
- You are asked to train others to do your job.
- Management asks you to track *all* your time.
- An overall feeling of tension from management is in the air.
- Management conducts off-site meetings, often involving odd hours, late nights, or weekends.
- You notice more than the usual number of early retirements or a string of retirements close to the end of the year. Multiple retirements, all within a similar period of time, often signal major changes (job losses, negative financial reports, policy/benefit changes, management changes).

Secure Signed and Approved Performance Reviews

- Your performance of "on-the-job responsibilities" is usually evaluated on an annual basis. As your review may go through multiple layers of management because of supervisory authority or required approval levels, you may not remember what was added, changed, or deleted. You need to get final copies of HR-filed evaluations with all signatures.
- Be sure to capture your real performance numbers, especially if you are forced to downgrade your performance because of an implied or verbal bell curve or "off-the-record" salary or performance rating controls.
- Maintain copies of annual performance reviews and key documents highlighting your accomplishments and recognitions. This will give you the vital information needed to build your résumé without wasting time requesting copies from HR as an former employee.

Secure Copies of Your Contact Base

- Maintain copies of your database at home. (Make sure this is not a violation of your company's policy.) If copying your contact database is against company policy, create a spreadsheet with the information you will need to contact outside vendors, coworkers, and any other person who may be able to help you in the future.

Secure All "Atta-Boy" Emails or Other Positive Performance Notes

- Get into the habit of sending copies of congratulatory emails you receive to your home address, especially if the email shows proactive behavior or quantifiable, measurable benefits that may not show up in your annual performance review.
- This ensures you will have informational emails when you need them and eliminates the struggle of pulling multiple emails together when you are the victim of corporate flattening.

Secure the Latest Version of Your Company's Employee Handbook

- Now, *read it*. Focus on job loss policies, benefits, and procedures.
- Familiarize yourself with policies on outplacement and job loss benefits offered to employees.

- Remember that revisions to the employee handbook regarding changes to severance benefits are often an indication that downsizing is coming.

Request Up-to-Date Pension Plan Information and Statements
- Ensure you will be paid pension benefits and that you will continue to be eligible for benefits if the company is sold in the future.
- Confirm your understanding of pension benefits and eligibility by sending a thank-you note summarizing your conversation with appropriate people.

Clarify Your Retirement Benefits (and Funds Paid into Your Retirement Account)
- Obtain copies of your retirement benefits.
- Confirm your individual retirement account is portable. When you leave the company you will (most probably) want to roll over your retirement account so you have control and can manage it.
- Contact your financial adviser to discuss options in advance of a potential downsizing.

Gather Copies of Your Best Work, Company Recognitions, and Useful Reports
- Create a portfolio of your best work, which means work that exceeds normal, measurable expectations. Include projects that were new and profitable (because of input you provided) and samples or pictures of finished work. Make notations as to what was important and different. Describe the long-term impact of your contribution—to the product, to the team, to the department, and to the overall profitability of the company.
- Blind copy to yourself (not at your workplace), your best work, company recognition for your work, and any important data that will be useful in creating your résumé.

Slowly Remove Personal Items from Your Cube or Office
- By taking personal items home early, you ensure that important items will not be lost or misdirected. Once the "ax falls," you will lose

control of your space, so early (and slow) removal of your personal items eliminates the loss of any items or the inconvenience of having to track what is not returned to you. In many cases, this will also eliminate the need to make an appointment with security to return after hours to pack an entire career's worth of possessions.

- If you do lose your job, there is a strong likelihood you will be escorted back to your cube by an HR or a security person to get your keys before you are led out the door. You can avoid this public humiliation in front of your peers by taking your keys with you. It is time to put your keys in your pocket when you: (1) are working in the company intranet and suddenly get "knocked off," (2) try to log into your company e-mail and your password does not work, (3) receive a call to report to your managers office, or (4) look up and see your immediate supervisor in front of your cube.
- If you are not affected by the rumored downsizing, you can always bring back your personal items.

Create a Packing List of all Remaining Personal Items of Value

- Snap a picture of your office (with your cell phone/camera) showing large personal items (e.g., lamps, plants, small appliances, chairs, framed pictures) that are too heavy and noticeable to move prior to your being laid off. This will document your belongings.
- Label all large or bulky items, as well as all remaining personal pieces, with your name and contact information, including cell phone number.
- Maintain a packing list to ensure all items are returned to you. Often, layoff survivors "swoop in" and confiscate items left in your workspace for their benefit.

Day of the Layoff: The Ax Has Dropped

Have you planned ahead . . . organized yourself . . . checked off your "to-do" list? *Recheck!*

Observations on the Day of the Layoff

- Twice the number of guards, some of whom may be carrying firearms
- Company parking lots patrolled by more security cars than usual or even by cars from a different and private security company
- Police cars parked by the company gates or exits
- Coworkers huddling in the break room or by the water cooler whispering and looking stressed out
- Coworkers staying in their workspaces trying to look busy and hoping not to be part of the layoff process
- Unusual movement of guards walking the floors, observing what's happening

Don't Let Security Intimidate You

- As you are stripped of all company identity, you may be astonished to find that you are now considered a risk to the company. Security wants you out of the building as quickly as possible to prevent (in its eyes) any retaliation, vandalism, or property damage.
- You may feel you're being treated like a criminal, but stay in control of the situation and maintain your dignity and professionalism with a smile.

Remember that you do not want to "burn any bridges," especially when you may need to retrieve the remainder of your personal items, secure company documents or forms, and retain that ever-so-important severance package.

Secure from Human Resources a Current Certificate of Health Insurance
If you can do this earlier rather than later, the better this will be.

- This certificate is critical to ensure you still have company coverage under the healthcare plan.
- The Certificate of Health Benefits of Insurability guarantees that your new company will not exclude you from coverage of extenuating conditions (e.g., high blood pressure, diabetes) or other preexisting

healthcare concerns. If you fail to request this documentation, pre-existing conditions may be excluded from future healthcare coverage, and you may have to reapply for and/or reestablish medical confirmation for such conditions.

- Even with the President's new healthcare mandate, this documentation may help speed your transition to new healthcare coverage.

Do Not Sign Your Severance Package at the Time of Your Termination

- You will have thirty days to review all paperwork given to you for your signature.

First Days After Your Job Loss

What just hit you? Are you dreaming? Is this reality? *Take a deep breath!*

Expect to Feel Numb/In a Daze

- Even if you are prepared for a layoff mentally, it is almost impossible to know how you will feel and react emotionally. Feeling numb, disoriented, or dazed is common because your mind and body are still not processing the life-changing event that has just occurred.
- Go easy on yourself and allow time to adjust to what is a new period in your life.
- You may also feel relief that the downsizing has happened; you may be glad the wait is finally over.

Do Not Make Any Life-Changing Decisions

- Do not panic or make long-term decisions like selling your house, car, or any other major investment. First you need to manage the many short-term issues/concerns that confront you.

Understand the Overall Emotional Impact of Job Loss

- To acknowledge the bitter realities of being out of work takes time. Unlike other life-changing events (like the loss of a loved one), there are no socially acceptable rituals to follow after losing your job.

- It is common to feel abandoned, alone, and in shock.
- Don't expect emotional support from your former coworkers (who were fortunate enough to survive the layoff/downsize). They have had to pick up your workload and are stressed (fearful) about losing their jobs in the future. Your former company goes on without you. It "is" what it "is."

Hot Flash of Emotions

- As you move through the initial disbelief of losing your job, it is important to understand the Emotional Wave of Unemployment and effectively control your feelings as you move into the job search mode of reality.

Understand the 7 Stages of the Emotional Wave of Unemployment

I'll go into more detail on the Emotional Wave of Unemployment in Chapter 1. For now here's a quick look at the seven stages of job loss grief you will encounter when you are forced to leave a job (see Exhibit P-1).

Stage 1: Shock and Denial

- Even as you look back on your layoff/downsizing, you may continue to feel as if you are in a fog—as if the entire experience is unreal, untrue, and not happening to you.
- This is not the time to act irrationally by sending out old résumés, writing or blogging about how badly you were treated, or telling people what you really think of your former company.
- You may be overwhelmed by humiliation and shame. These feelings will pass with time and as you begin your job search.

Stage 2: Fear and Panic

- Schedule a daily "worry time." When you catch yourself worrying, remind yourself your worry time is scheduled from ____ to ____ and that you have other more important things to do.

Exhibit P-1   Emotional Wave of Unemployment

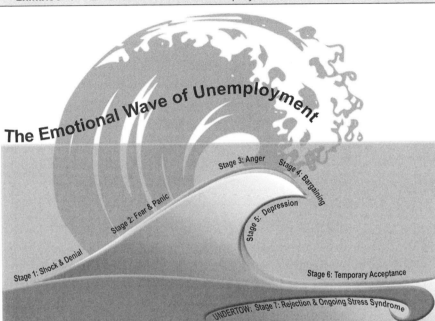

The Emotional Wave of Unemployment

Stage 3: Anger
Stage 4: Bargaining
Stage 2: Fear & Panic
Stage 5: Depression
Stage 1: Shock & Denial
Stage 6: Temporary Acceptance
UNDERTOW: Stage 7: Rejection & Ongoing Stress Syndrome

Illustration by Candace Smith ©2013

- Fight the feelings of scarcity that will arise as you manage the fear of losing everything. Create a list that prioritizes ongoing expenses and compare those items with your anticipated income. By creating an expense spreadsheet, you will get a broad view of how much you can afford to spend and will be able to determine which expenses are necessities, which can be eliminated, and which involve luxuries that need to be postponed to a later day. Figure out what you can do now for less money. This process gives you a reality check and helps prioritize life goals.
  - Be sure to include one-time expenses, such as annual taxes (and taxes on a pension's lump sum payout if you receive one).
- Train yourself to fight scarcity by teaching yourself to say, "We may not be able to afford XX, but we can afford YY instead."

Stage 3: Coping with Anger

- Learn to channel your anger. Constructively channeled anger will energize your job search.
- Anger, turned inward, creates depression, which can result in dark places in your life that make you feel out of control and not a part of life's cycle.
- Remember that unexpressed anger, not channeled or controlled, often turns into rage and ends up hurting others as well as yourself.
- Get physical—walk, run, jog, swim, beat sofa cushions. . . . Do anything appropriate to safely vent your anger.
- Avoid, if possible, criticizing or expressing your feelings about your former company (especially when in public places). You never know what stranger, in hearing range, may have some connection with your former company or whose family or friends may work there. Words once spoken or written are very difficult to take back.

Stage 4: Bargaining

- After extinguishing your anger, your mind may temporarily go blank and the desire to fight back (perhaps wanting revenge) will creep in.
- You may be convinced that a former coworker, vendor, family member, friend, or someone they know will become your "job savior" and find a new position for you.
- You may make exaggerated promises to yourself, but this is only a bargaining game within your head. Like—"When I get a job, I will work ten-hour days, seven days a week; without complaints." The reality is you just want to work again.

Stage 5: Depression

- Once you realize that bargaining with yourself, as well as with anyone else, won't get your job back, despair and depression may overwhelm you.
- Note that throughout your job search, you will experience the rollercoaster highs and lows (depression) of finding a new job. Don't let depression (feelings of guilt and worthlessness) overtake your

determination to find a new beginning (with good feelings). Ask for professional help if you feel you are becoming clinically depressed.

- Forgive yourself, the company that downsized you, your boss and coworkers, and any others who may have hurt you. It is very hard, but necessary, to forgive to avoid long-term depression.
- Volunteer because being productive feels good and allows you to focus on what you have instead of what you lost. Volunteering gets you out of the house and back into the stream of life.

Stage 6: Temporary Acceptance

- Acceptance gives you breathing room to plan. Like all stages in this emotional wave, acceptance of job loss is fluid and temporary. Use this time to prepare yourself for your job search.
- Temporary acceptance gives you a chance to pause. Get up—shake yourself off—and make the decision to *move on*. However difficult it may be, life does go on. You may find yourself experiencing temporary acceptance in different phases of your job search, especially when you experience Stage 7, which is rejection, but only you can make the decision to push on and get through this stage of your life.

Stage 7: Rejection

- Less than 20 percent of all jobs are found on the Internet, in newspapers, or at job fairs. All these sources are very impersonal.
  - People rarely acknowledge online applications, most of which are impossible to follow up.
  - After you spend hours online completing an application, the company will often "park" your application on its server—unread. It may sit there for weeks while others are reviewed and rejected just because your application did not contain the computerized, identified keywords. Thus, your application has fallen into a "black hole" and you hear nothing.

What follows are days, weeks, months, and sometimes even years working to fit back into the world of employability—to find that next job opportunity and get on with your life. With the help of hundreds of competent professionals who have endured periods of unemployment, a 7-Step Job Search Checklist has been developed, which covers everything from the initial break from gainful employment → to accepting the break up → to redesigning yourself as a job search candidate → to marketing this new professional image with added confidence and perseverance → to confidently finding your next job opportunity → to finally getting back into the employment market.

CHECKLIST

Prequels—Days Before . . . Day of . . . Days After

_____ Organize yourself.

_____ Maintain your dignity and reputation.

_____ *Do not* sign anything until you have had time to adjust to your job loss.

_____ Understand your compensation package.

_____ Obtain legal assistance (if needed).

_____ Inform your family.

_____ Understand the Emotional Wave of Unemployment.

REMAIN POSITIVE ABOUT YOURSELF

The Emotional Impact of Job Loss

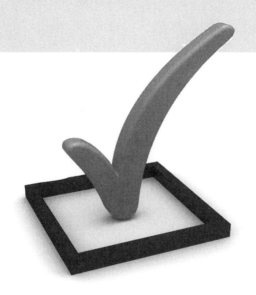

CHECKLIST

____   Understanding the emotional wave of employment.
____   Hidden family issues—helping family members cope.
____   Redefining family relationships—you are in this together!
____   Fighting feelings of scarcity—finances taking center stage.
____   Temporary changes—responding to a new economic reality.
____   Feelings of powerlessness—be patient.
____   Creating low cost/no cost alternatives.

Job Loss Grieving

For me, the most difficult part of being downsized was the intense job loss flashbacks. I would be in the middle of applying for a job, on a follow-up phone call, or emailing; then (out of nowhere), I would flash back to the moment of my job loss. All of the intense emotions of losing my job would then follow—the shame and humiliation, the shock and denial, the fear and the panic, the bitterness and anger, and, on some days, the depression. I was ready to lash out, wanting to even the score with my old company in any way possible.

Resentment and anger drove me to build a small model boat that had plenty of room for all my "outstanding company" awards and a special place for a powerful cylindrical firecracker (left over from the 4th of July). I took one last look at my awards, lit the long fuse, and pushed the model boat quickly away from the shore. Soon a mushroom cloud of water erupted and all traces of my award-winning professional life were obliterated and slowly sank into the lake. It provided immense relief, but the next day my feelings of abandonment, discouragement, emptiness, and hopelessness were still there, along with the reality of being unemployed.

Why Is Job Loss Like an Emotional Wave?

Job loss grieving follows an Emotional Wave of Unemployment (or E-Wave) because without planning or permission, you are dumped into an ocean of emotions—shock and denial, fear and panic, anger, depression, and temporary acceptance. Just when you think you may have bottomed out, rejection creates one more wave you need to navigate.

Job loss grieving is a normal process people go through, although not everyone encounters all of the above stages. Losing a job is traumatic and devastating because there are no socially acceptable rituals to follow. Job loss is complicated and changes your life. People may not be able to see it, but you have been badly bruised on the inside. Still, you are expected to be strong on the outside.

Some people know in advance that downsizing is impending. They recognize the signs of layoffs, hear rumors that the company is going out of business, or simply work in a company that has constant turn over of personnel. They may take early retirement or start preparing well before the layoffs take effect. These individuals have the chance to process job loss on their time and terms and actually may be relieved when a final downsize or release occurs.

Once you understand the emotional stages of job loss grieving, you can better cope with the process. This chapter reviews each of the emotional stages of unemployment and provides proven strategies for conquering the loss. In addition, it discusses the potential impact of posttraumatic stress, the ongoing stress of being out of work, and how this stress may impact your ability to find a job.

Stage 1: Shock and Denial

Remember when you heard the words "Your position has been eliminated" plus all the other noise you heard ("blah, blah, blah") from thereon, but didn't absorb, only to hear again "I am sure you understand. . . . Mary from HR is going to introduce you to 'blah, blah, blah,' who will help you find another job. 'blah, blah, blah' 'Good Luck.' . . . ."

Like so many others in your company who have been terminated, you have just gone into shock. Even if you believed the rumors, you didn't think the layoffs would affect you because you have:

- Always done the "right thing."
- Worked overtime without complaint.

- Postponed vacations when asked.
- Always thought it would be someone else.

And, like most people, you probably said to yourself:

- How could this happen to me?
- This must be a mistake!
- My professional life is over.
- What will I tell my spouse and children?

The public announcement of your termination may not seem real and, at the time, nothing else will either. People have told me over the years that they felt like zombies in a bad movie . . . this is your mind going into shock.

Coping with Shock and Denial

Give yourself plenty of time and the privacy needed to recuperate. Fight the urge to blast your former employer on Facebook or Twitter. This is *not* the time to post anything on any public forum, write letters, call people, or broadcast the news of your termination. Instead, begin to think about your options and plan your next steps. Pamper yourself by allowing time for you to catch your breath, pause, and then proceed.

Stage 2: Fear and Panic

When I was out of work, I began to believe that everywhere I went people were looking at me. At one point, I thought the word "loser" had been tattooed on my forehead or "will work for food" was written on my chest. During the day, I didn't answer my door or telephone or go outside. I didn't want my neighbors to know I was out of a job and at home.

Fear and panic can create a sense of anxiety. Relatively minor decisions and events can sometimes become enormous and frightening.

A member of Professionals in Transition® Support Group Inc. (PIT®) once shared how she obsessed about the air conditioner in her house coming on when she was out of work. "Whenever the blower came on, I thought of the expense. How long will it run? How much will it cost?" To regain control and reduce costs, she turned down the air conditioner and began sweating to save money.

Anything that costs money during unemployment brings up a host of valid concerns. During the fear and panic stage, you may spend much of your time and energy obsessed on concerns such as:

- Will I have to declare bankruptcy?
- What happens if I lose everything I own?
- Will my family and friends abandon me?
- Is this the end of my career?
- Will any employer ever give me another chance?

Fear and panic may also lead to indecisiveness. Every minor choice may take on an exaggerated importance and sometimes may make you feel as if the world will end if an incorrect decision is made. For example, Rick, who lost his job as a bank teller, remembers how much of an ordeal it was for him to figure out how to present himself on job interviews. "I'd change my tie ten times, and then go back to the one I had originally chosen." Each time he hesitated, Rick felt as though his indecision proved he was a loser and reinforced his inability to follow his own trusted instincts.

Fear, panic, and indecision are appropriate responses to losing your job. Nothing could be more natural than to worry about the future when your income and career have just been stolen and you don't know what tomorrow will bring.

Coping with Fear and Panic

The key to managing fear and panic is to put your concerns into perspective. Create a scheduled worry time. When I caught myself worrying outside of my worry time, I would tell myself "*You can't worry now because your worry time isn't until 2:00 this afternoon.*" Did it stop me from worrying? Sometimes, but mostly it reminded me to relax, take a deep breath, and keep moving forward.

A feeling of scarcity may envelop you and your family. This is a very common reaction to losing a job. What is interesting is the "scarcity mentality" touches all income levels. It makes no difference if you are a newly created "golden-parachute" executive or a factory worker. During job loss, fear is an appropriate response because your identity and income have been "jerked" away. To reduce fear, choose, instead, to move forward. Know that there is another job for you out there; positive thinking always helps change your situation.

Begin to control fear and panic (and the scarcity mentality) by creating a prioritized list of all outgoing expenses and compare that list with incoming monies, including severance, dividends, and unemployment benefits (see Exhibit 1-1). Now is the time to be proactive and make adjustments.

Ongoing expenses (nonnegotiable items) include:

- Food
- Utilities
- Housing
- Childcare
- Healthcare
- Taxes

One time/current (nonnegotiable) expenses include:

- Health club or gym. Let someone in charge know your situation. The club may not charge you (or may reduce your membership fee) while you are unemployed. Physical exercise reduces stress and gives you the chance to think, so you want to keep your membership if possible.
- If you have planned and partially paid for a vacation, take it. The cancellation fees alone may eliminate any savings you would have been able to reclaim. Instead, call the companies, explain your situation, and see if you can negotiate a lower cost version of your trip. Vacation renegotiation may eliminate the need for you to pay the remaining portion of the deposit.
- If your kids have been promised summer camps and you have prepaid, let them go.
- Maintain as many family rituals as possible, but don't be afraid to modify them to meet your new budget. Maintaining an attitude of abundance instead of scarcity may seem *contrary to* common sense,

(text continues on page 28)

Exhibit 1-1   Evaluating Finances

TOTAL MONTHLY FIXED EXPENSES

Ongoing costs: Expenses you may need to pay each month

	Current Monthly	Revised Monthly
Rent/Mortgage/Property Taxes		
Personal Taxes (Vehicles)		
Gas/Electric/Water (Utilities)		
Telephone/Cable		
Insurance: Automobile		
Health		
Life		
Credit Payments: Loans		
Credit Cards		
Retail Cards		
Childcare		
Other		
TOTAL FIXED EXPENSES		

TOTAL MONTHLY VARIABLE EXPENSES

Unnecessary costs: Items for which you may have allocated funds, but which could be cut back if needed. The "current" column should contain the amount which you are currently spending. The "revised" column can be completed later to reflect those expenses that have been revised downward.

	Current Monthly	Revised Monthly
Food: Groceries		
Eating Out		
Clothing: New Purchases		
Dry Cleaning		
Transportation: Gasoline		
Parking/Public		
Maintenance: Vehicles		
Recreation: Entertainment		
Publications		

Education: Tuition		
Supplies		
Charitable Contributions		
Personal Items		
TOTAL VARIABLE EXPENSES		

NET INCOME – List your monthly sources of net income (after taxes)

	Current Monthly	Revised Monthly
Salary/Wages/Severance Pay		
Part-Time Jobs		
Unemployment Benefits		
Commissions		
Secondary Income (Spouse Income)		
Rental Properties		
Investments		
Other		
TOTAL Monthly Net Income		

BUDGET SUMMARY

Subtract Monthly Fixed Expenses/Monthly Variable Expenses from Total Monthly Net Income.

	Total Monthly Net Income	_____
Less:	**Total Monthly Fixed Expenses**	_____
Less:	**Total Monthly Variable Expenses**	_____
	NET MONTHLY DIFFERENCE	_____

If you have a net monthly surplus, you are in good shape. If, however, your monthly difference is a negative, you need to consider reducing expenditures to equalize your income and expenses.

(continues)

Exhibit 1-1 *(continued)*
1. Be more conscious of utility expenditures, telephone contracts, and cable contracts (reduce if necessary).
2. Be conscious of extra spending (clothing, accessories, luxury items).
   Pay with cash instead of credit cards.
   Be cautious of late fees (contact your credit card provider and negotiate).
3. Liquidate excessive assets (only as last resort).

but with some creativity tempered by the new realities of your budget, you will be able to replicate many of your family and personal activities.

You will also reduce personal guilt and anxiety by teaching yourself to say: "*We can afford to do this instead.*" By looking at the situation in a positive manner, your outlook will feel different. Your ability to find creative ways around the temporary inconvenience of being unemployed will help create breathing room as you begin to rebuild your professional identity. (See Chapter 5, "Rebuilding Your Professional Identity")

Notify your bank and all other creditors of your new situation. Let them know you will be paying the minimum amount due each month. By sharing this information, you are making debtors your *partners not* your enemies. Putting all of this in writing reestablishes personal control and reduces some stress. More importantly, it creates a paper trail of your good intent and may open a channel of communication between you and your creditors.

If you're having trouble making decisions, limit the time you give yourself to choose. Allow yourself one minute to make a forced choice. This prevents you from being paralyzed over small decisions that used to be a snap to make. Few choices are of the "forever" variety. In all likelihood, you'll get a chance to resolve any potential mistake you make along the way.

Stage 3: Anger

Anger is an appropriate response to job loss. It lingers just below the surface and can well up unexpectedly. Once when shopping, I ran into a former coworker. For an instant, our eyes met. Then, she quickly went down the next aisle trying to avoid me. I felt angry that she could be so thoughtless, although it made sense she would feel awkward and not know what to say to me.

Righteous anger tends to explode, and you may find yourself screaming:

- This isn't fair!
- How can they do this to me?
- This is an outrage!
- They have no right!

Because there's no effective way to vent your rage, anger can and will build up inside of you. The longer you think (stew) about your situation, the angrier and more resentful you will become. You want to even the score, lash out, and wipe that smug look off their faces.

The trick is to manage anger by channeling it. Anger is the fire in your belly. Properly channeled, it will energize your job search. Harness the anger and let it propel you forward into positive reemployment-based activities.

If you push down the anger instead of channeling it, the anger will fester and continue to gnaw at you. Tamped-down anger can morph into depression. Unexpressed anger can be heard in your voice and impact how you interview. Anger can destroy relationships, while distancing family and friends.

Coping with Anger

The most important thing is getting anger out; how you do it is up to you. Your body will take the liberty of translating your emotions into physical symptoms. Why not take advantage of those building emotions by directing that powerful negative energy into your job search? I had a friend who installed a punching bag in his basement. Every time he got angry, he put on his gloves and imagined the punching bag was the face of his old boss. After pounding his former boss to smithereens, my friend would then continue his job search in a much more relaxed frame of mind.

Channel your emotions by doing something physical: go for a walk/run, work out, swim, or go to the soccer field and kick goals until you're exhausted. Don't be afraid to tackle your "to-do" list, including home improvement projects, or your "wish" list, including learning new skills such as cooking/baking/cake decorating. Smash things (without harming yourself or anyone else), beat sofa cushions, or have a pillow fight. Do anything to vent and redirect your anger into positive energy. Redirecting your emotions and mind helps refocus current happenings and puts you back in control of your thoughts, reenergizes your spirit, and helps you to move forward in different directions of *your choice.*

What you *shouldn't* do is contain your anger or vent it at the wrong times or in the wrong places. Avoid the temptation to blast your old company and former employer in public because an angry person is perceived as unemployable. Remember that unexpressed anger is unhealthy, as it will grow into rage, which ends up harming you in more than one way.

Stage 4: Bargaining

Once you've expressed your anger, you will be exhausted. Your mind may go blank or the desire to fight and get revenge will temporarily disappear. Instead, you may become convinced that the job savior will appear and make all the pain disappear. Thoughts similar to the following may occur to you:

- I'll get another job right away.
- Maybe it was all a mistake.
- The situation can't be as bad as it seems.
- Maybe my old company will apologize and take me back when management sees what a mistake it was to let me go.

You bargain with yourself that if your former boss rehires you or another job appears, you will never borrow another company-bought pencil or you will work ten hours a day/six days a week without complaint. You promise to learn from your mistakes and become the worthiest employee, family member, and world citizen.

During the bargaining stage, you may begin to fantasize that a quick and painless ending to your unemployment crisis will happen soon. Thoughts such as the following may enter your mind: I'm sure my buddy, Bob, will keep his word and help me find a job because "he promised to help" or "All I have to do is learn the latest software program and my phone will ring off the hook."

In your attempt to make the pain go away, you may continue to wait for the job savior. People kept telling me what a great person I was and reassuring me I would have no problem finding a job. The first time I was out of work, I exhausted my frequent flier miles traveling across the country to attend a trade event and hand out résumés like a paper boy. I said to every vendor I met, "I just lost my job, can you help me out?" I was absolutely convinced my next employer was at the trade event and that someone from the industry would create the perfect job for me. Five hundred résumés, 50 follow-up letters, 4 job interviews, and no job later, I realized there *was* no such thing as a job savior. I learned the hard way that my full-time job now was finding a full-time job.

Coping with Bargaining

One of the most shocking things about job loss is that you learn very quickly who your true friends are and who your work acquaintances *were*. It is a bitter pill to swallow. Thinking there is somebody out there who's going to swoop into your life and eliminate the job loss pain is a comforting thought, but in more than 95 percent of cases, this just doesn't happen.

Stage 5: Depression

Once you realize that bargaining won't get your old boss to reverse his decision, despair may set in. Feeling abandoned is natural when you consider your routine, status, professional network, workstation, lunch group, and even your water cooler chat group has been eliminated from your life. You may find that every mistake you may have made, every skeleton in your closet, and even unresolved issues from your past come bubbling to the surface of your consciousness.

Here are some of the thoughts that may creep into your mind:

- It's all my fault.
- My best days are gone.
- If only I had done X instead of Y, they may not have let me go.
- I will never get another job.
- This is the end of the road for me.

Depression is anger turned inward. I vividly imagined myself sitting on a park bench, unshaven. In my mind's eye, my clothes were tattered. I was holding a half-empty bottle of cheap, convenience store wine. My car had been repossessed, and my wife and kids had left me. And, I knew I'd earned every bit of what was happening to me.

When I really got down, all I wanted to do was sleep. I stopped answering the phone, didn't go outside, and basically gave up on life. People would knock on the door, and I wouldn't answer. I had no energy or desire to job search. I felt stupid and ashamed for losing my job, and I just wanted to hide and be left alone.

Be prepared to hit bottom, perhaps even more than once. Battling depression can become a daily occurrence. If you are depressed, understand that it can be the result of a chemical imbalance in your body. It is not your fault and can be treated with medication. If depression is a recurring emotion for you, seek immediate professional help. But, if depression has not completely overwhelmed you, there are proven techniques you can use to convert depression into action.

Coping with Depression

When job search depression takes over, you may be swamped with feelings of worthlessness, guilt, and lethargy. It may take all your energy just to get out of bed in the morning, so you have no strength left to fight your way out of the gloom. Depression can also be described as a cloud that blots out all your good feelings (especially about yourself).

Perhaps the hardest thing is to learn to forgive your former boss, your former employer, and even yourself for anything that may have happened in life. This is difficult to do and not something that occurs all at once. Self-forgiveness reduces the likelihood that you will criticize every move you make in the future. By forgiving your boss and the company you worked for, you enable yourself to move forward in your job search. Even though you have managed to forgive, you will never forget.

Now is the time to do all the things you never had time to do. Play with your kids, spend time with your spouse, take the time to laugh, and allow yourself to step outside of your job loss situation. Treat yourself as if you were your best friend.

Do something productive and helpful for other people. Volunteer to serve at a soup kitchen, clean up the litter in a local playground, or raise funds for your favorite charity. You will realize how much you have left to give and focus less on what you have lost.

Fight the fatigue that depression often brings. Remember that running, walking, swimming, and other aerobic activities energize you. Give yourself the chance to let loose, shake off the blues, and do something nice for your mind and body. Exercising will help you sleep better. An effective job search is most productive if you are rested and healthy, and your outlook is positive.

Stage 6: Temporary Acceptance

In the temporary acceptance stage, you pick yourself up, shake yourself off, and get on with life. You absolve yourself of blame for your unemployment and take charge of finding your next job. Although the crisis of unemployment is with you every moment of every day, you now have some breathing room. Some healthy concepts that begin to sink in are:

- The past is past, and it is time to move on.
- Life as a couch potato isn't doing me any good.
- I can't change anything by kicking myself in the butt.
- Why dwell on what I can't change?
- My job search is my responsibility, and I can make it happen.

Coping with Temporary Acceptance

If temporary acceptance were the final stop on the journey to your recovery, there'd be nothing to cope with. It would be time to celebrate. You'd be "over" the trauma of unemployment. However, job loss grieving is an emotional wave, a continual cycle and not a series of linear steps. You might accept your situation with grace one day and sink into depression the next. One minute you might be full of optimism; the next, you're heartbroken.

Be prepared to experience extreme mood swings as long as you're unemployed. Your feelings may be exaggerated. The highs will be much higher, and the lows much lower. What others may consider minor events—a rejection letter or a job application that you have invested hours online submitting but seemed to fall into the "black hole" of the Internet—can catapult you from the plateau of temporary acceptance to the depths of shock and denial, fear and panic, anger, bargaining, or depression.

Take advantage of temporary acceptance to prepare yourself for what lies ahead. Develop a plan and prepare to face the world again from the perspective of personal responsibility, forgiveness, and confidence.

Stage 7: Rejection

A job search is full of rejection. Positions you spend hours applying to online seem to disappear into a large black hole. Guess what? Many times they do! Because of the tremendous number of applications received, it is a common practice for an HR manager to "park" or hold applications until others are previewed and processed. Often, parked applications are never retrieved or seen by human eyes.

Hiring is simply a process and each company has its own approach. When you set your emotions aside and step outside of yourself, you will see that you are just an application in the eyes of the hiring company. Nothing personal is directed to you or your application. Just because you have not received a response does not mean you did anything wrong or that you are a failure. Remember that companies respond (or don't respond) on their timelines not yours.

Many times, your follow-up calls will go into a general HR voicemail, and emails and letters are often not answered. If you get no response, keep following through and try not to take it personally. When you get a promise of a callback from HR, it may be delayed for internal reasons. Fight rejection by sending a thank-you note to the person who called, summarizing the conversation and the next steps. Wait ten days, and call back.

Constant rejection is like big potholes that suddenly appear on the road to reemployment. They may temporarily knock you out of alignment. When it rains, it can (and often does) pour. Don't be surprised if unplanned issues and unexpected bills arrive at your doorstep. Each situation will stir up your feelings, seem like a major crisis, and throw you back into the emotional wave. Do your best, however, to manage these potholes and balance the whole picture. When you were employed, these issues were simply issues you handled. Regain control and approach each issue with different tactics until it is resolved or managed.

Coping with Rejection

Coping with rejection is an ongoing, daily process, so you must take things day by day. Be sure to create goals and measure daily productivity. Record your actual tasks, including:

- Positions applied for online.
- Follow-up calls made.
- Networking contacts activated.
- Research completed.

Manage rejection by using the Rule of 3/30. This means you follow through with potential networking opportunities, companies, and positions three times every month. When you do this, you will be following up every ten days, which is a balanced approach and does not seem desperate. Create a "No" list, on which it takes 99 rejections to get one yes. In my case, I was on #87 before I got another job.

End your job search in time for dinner, and do not return to it until the next day. When you go to bed each night, know that you did everything possible to find a job that day. Sleep well, as tomorrow is another day.

The Trauma of Job Loss and Understanding Stress

No hard-and-fast rule says everyone has to suffer from prolonged job loss grief. In most cases, however, unemployed individuals *do* find it necessary to learn how to manage rejection and all of the feelings encountered in the emotional wave of job loss before they can successfully move on with their professional lives.

Understanding stress and the possibility of job loss flashbacks is critical. This awareness will help you move beyond the paralysis brought on by downsizing.

I am not a board-certified mental health professional. My formal training is in business, psychology, and career counseling. I can only share with you what it was like for me and the thousands I have worked with over the past twenty years.

When I lost my job, my self-esteem evaporated. A strong professional identity and confidence were replaced by the dark clouds of insecurity, shame, and guilt. The intense weight of trying to figure out what to do next, along with the impact of the emotional wave, drowned my senses of hope and reality. Each time I lost my job, my experiences were violating, traumatic, and excruciating.

As I attempted to fight back against ongoing daily stress, rejections, and the similar feelings of helplessness, I came to relate these emotional job loss feelings to similar feelings of post delayed stress syndrome ("undertow" feelings of a different form).

Posttraumatic Stress Disorder (PTSD)

Posttraumatic Stress Disorder (PTSD) is a complex disorder in which the affected person's memory, emotional responses, intellectual processes, and nervous system have all been disrupted by one or more traumatic experiences. It is sometimes summarized as "a normal reaction to abnormal events"; a delayed stress reaction.[1]

Following a traumatic event, almost everyone experiences some degree of PTSD. When your sense of safety and trust have been shattered, it's normal to feel crazy, disconnected, or numb. It's common to have bad dreams, be fearful, and find it difficult to stop thinking about what happened.

For most people, these symptoms are short lived. They may last for several weeks or even months, but they gradually dissolve over time. These dreams usually disappear after you are back to work.

Individuals who suffer from PTSD find:

- Symptoms like flashbacks do not decrease.
- They do not feel better over time, but rather feel progressively feel worse.

If this is your case, please seek immediate professional help.[2]

Ongoing Traumatic Stress Disorder (OTSD)

In an article in *The Jewish Daily Forward* ("When It Comes to Being Unemployed"), Howard Fine wrote, "I — not being a mental health professional— am inclined to call PTSD, Ongoing Traumatic Stress Disorder (OTSD). . . . The National Institute of Mental Health comments, 'People may develop PTSD in reaction to events that may not qualify as traumatic, but can be devastating life events like divorce or unemployment.' For my part, I cannot imagine the feelings of helplessness these people suffer, nor the fears they experience as more and more states cut or propose to cut back on unemployment insurance payments and as more and more of them lose their homes to foreclosure."[3]

PTSD and OTSD Play a Dual Role in Job Loss Grieving

I believe that *both* PTSD and OTSD play a role in job loss grieving. The symptoms that define PTSD must last more than a month and may include:

- Recurrent, intrusive, distressing dreams and memories of a trauma
- Frequent flashbacks triggering a frame-by-frame review of your job loss.
- Extreme distress or trigger events that in some way symbolize or resemble your job loss experience, including:
  - Unemployment stories in the news media
  - Announcements of other layoffs
  - Friends who lose their jobs after you

- ○ Unexpected bills or expenses
- ○ Family or life events that normally would not cause a traumatic stress reaction
- Attempting to avoid thoughts, feelings, and activities associated with the event
- Inability to remember important details
- Feelings of detachment and estrangement from loved ones
- Insomnia
- Extreme irritability
- Inability to concentrate
- Hypervigilance or an exaggerated startle response

Many of us have experienced trauma. With major changes in the economic markets, circumstances can trigger memories and/or experiences of individual feelings of confusion, pain, and loss of control. If you're experiencing any of these symptoms, reach out for help. Don't assume you can handle the problems yourself. We all go through stressful times, and it's good to have support when we need it.

Ongoing Traumatic Stress Disorder (OTSD) symptoms can be identical to PTSD symptoms. When you combine the personal and emotional components of job loss grieving with the ongoing stress that unemployment brings to you and your family, identical symptoms can affect you physically, mentally, and psychologically.

My research indicates that the terms Posttraumatic Stress Disorder (PTSD) and Ongoing Traumatic Stress Disorder (OTSD) have been used interchangeably to describe the symptoms of traumatic stress. What does this mean to you? By understanding the impact of job loss, you will be able to:

- Anticipate and cope with each stage of the emotional wave.
- Manage the ongoing stress of job searching.
- Become aware of PTSD and OTSD and the importance of recognizing and reacting to the symptoms.

If you feel you have any of the above or similar indicators of PTSD or OTSD, seek additional support through special support counseling groups, such as Family Services or the Veterans Administration, or with someone in your religious organization with whom you are comfortable talking.

CHECKLIST

Chapter 1—Job Loss Grieving

_____ Are you organized and ready to start this journey back into employment?

_____ Do you understand the Emotional Wave of Unemployment and the possible undertow emotions?

_____ Do you feel you need professional counseling to understand your feelings or emotions?

Have you empowered yourself:

     _____ To start again?

     _____ To remain positive about yourself?

     _____ To communicate with others?

     _____ To change the things you can?

_____ Do you remember not to send out your résumé until you understand your professional identity and develop your marketing plans.

Secondhand Job Loss

Job loss shakes you to the very core of your being. In addition to stripping away your professional identity, it inflicts secondhand loss on loved ones. In most cases, they feel what you feel—only at different times.

The most frustrating part for family members is only being able to watch you go through the job search process. The longer your job loss goes on, the more frustrating it becomes for family members, and the more difficult it becomes for you. Family members experience secondhand job loss because they cannot find a job for you; they can only sit on the sidelines and watch your hopes rise and fall with each application or job interview. Their frustration builds as a result of their love and concern for you.

When you're out of work, any hidden family issues that may have existed in your household will tend to be magnified. At best, unemployment can become a stimulus for change and an opportunity to resolve issues that may have been simmering on the back burner for years. At worst, unemployment can crack a family's foundation and become the catalyst for failure. A steady income creates security. When job security is blasted to smithereens, unresolved problems in domestic relationships can bubble up. For example, if you have had trouble communicating with family members in the past, unemployment will aggravate this tendency and likely make it even more difficult to talk openly.

You're in It Together

If your family was tenuously held together by money or the prestige associated with your position, now is the time to redefine the relationship. This means creating a "grounding force" while you're unemployed. Your significant other, children, and close relatives can help you keep problems in perspective by reminding you that *life exists beyond business* and ensuring that you don't have to face the uncertain future alone. Your family can help provide the stability and continuity you crave while you're unemployed and as you make the transition to a new job. In return, you can help your significant other, children, and relatives cope with the short-term changes they face while you are seeking reemployment. Creating a solid foundation can maximize your family's chances of emerging from the reemployment experience whole and ready to face together whatever challenges and opportunities lie ahead.

To support your loved ones while you are unemployed, pay attention to what they are experiencing. That means making an effort to ask how everyone is feeling and what you can do to help regardless of what you're going through. Don't assume your family members' concerns and emotions will be in sync with yours.

Keep in mind the special ways in which unemployment affects your children. Young children will probably not understand enough about your job to react in the same way as adult members of your household. That doesn't mean they will be untouched or unaffected by your unemployment. On the contrary, your children will feel the anxiety and tension that prevails in your home, and they will hear adults whispering in worried tones. This may trigger adult emotional reactions, such as fear and panic. As a result, your children will need your continuous love, reassurance, and guidance as much as, if not more than, the adults in your household. Take the time to offer an age-appropriate explanation of your job loss. Emphasize the fact that any consequences of your unemployment will be short lived and that, together, the family can handle any problems that arise.

Fighting Scarcity

Job loss creates an immediate sense of scarcity regardless of your income level. Finances take center stage; expenses that never worried you before will suddenly become a big deal. How will you pay the mortgage or keep up with your insurance or utility bills? Luxuries you could afford last week—dining out, vacations, summer camp, and similar enjoyments—will, of necessity, need to be reviewed and possibly eliminated.

In addition, you may feel that your established role in the family is threatened. If you were the breadwinner and you temporarily can't provide for your loved ones (at least in the manner to which they have been accustomed), members of your household can suffer a crisis of faith. For the same reasons, your self-esteem can take a nose dive, and you are likely to be overwhelmed with guilt. To make matters worse, if you're suddenly around the house most of the time when you were traditionally unobtrusive or even somewhat "invisible," you may suddenly find yourself in the way. You may even find yourself feeling like "dead weight" or the family's "fifth wheel." In addition, you may experience overwhelming embarrassment and shame because of what your family is now being forced to deal with.

Regardless of the details, your family will have to manage a host of temporary changes and that will pose challenges for everyone. If you understand the issues that are likely to arise—particularly your family's feelings of "powerlessness" and the "rising tensions" in your household—and prepare yourself to handle them, you will be well on your way toward successfully guiding your family through the reemployment process.

Powerlessness

Your significant other and children's immediate grief may, in many cases, be less intense than yours. Unemployment will create ups and downs in their lives just as it will in yours, but it is you, not your family, who has been cast out from the working world. Your professional routine has been shattered, and you, not your family, will have to redefine and reengineer your career identity. Although your family members and friends can try to commiserate with you, they are grieving your job loss "secondhand." They too are experiencing sudden upheaval and uncertainty in their lives, but unlike you, their daily routine and overall identities have not been personally violated.

Because they are on the periphery of your job loss, they may also feel a sense of helplessness. They have no control over the reemployment process and can only watch as you call the shots. Family members may feel powerless, as they can only watch from the sidelines and provide support. They may become frustrated—for you—as you learn daily about reemployment through trial and error. Job search dead ends and mistakes are a part of the frustrating process of finding a job. Knowing this in the beginning of the reemployment process can go a long way toward helping everyone in the family cope.

In addition, their lack of control over your job search may leave them frightened and angry. To counter your family's feelings of powerlessness, find ways to put them in the driver's seat as much as possible. Here are some approaches to consider:

- Make your significant other a total fiscal partner. Look at the family's income and expenses and realistically assess your financial picture together. Start by adjusting your budget. Decide with your significant other which luxuries you can postpone, reduce the cost of, or temporarily eliminate. At the same time, determine the "nonnegotiable items" you will maintain at all costs. Once you have determined what goes and what absolutely has to stay, begin working toward eliminating things in the middle. Consider this middle ground as "nice to have, but not needing to have." The key to proactive budget analysis and planning is to include your significant other as a co-decision maker for all of the issues involving the household's finances.
- Set new priorities for your family's remaining income. When you've agreed on a plan, share it with your children and answer their questions about the immediate situation and the short-term future. By making the new budget a family project, members will feel a sense of control as together the family confronts the challenge of reduced cash flow.

- Assign measurable, money-saving tasks to family members. For example: Older children might wash the car or mow the lawn; younger children might be responsible for clipping coupons or turning off lights in empty rooms. Let your children know how much their efforts contribute to the family's savings.
- Solicit your family's help in creating no-cost, appealing substitutes for the pleasures you are no longer able to afford. Instead of eating out, prepare nutritious low-cost, homemade meals; utilize NetFlix®, Red Box®, or DVDs at home instead of supporting the local theater conglomerate.

Managing Family Tension

Sometimes, even minor irritations can erupt into significant conflicts. Small things, like failing to take out the trash or leaving the dishes in the sink, can become focal points of ferocious battles. Job loss is already stressful. Try not to wage major battles over minor things.

Tension reveals itself in other ways too. You may begin to feel jealous of a significant other who goes off to work every day and leaves you behind to wallow in your misery.

Your kids too can unintentionally hurt you by requesting things you can no longer afford or reminding you of broken promises (such as a canceled vacation). But all the tension in your household doesn't originate with others; some of it begins with you.

Try a couple of these "tension busters" to stem the negative effects of rising tension in your household:

- Talk with your family and make sure everyone understands that unemployment is a temporary condition.
- Recognize and intervene when family members turn on each other. Sometimes the solution is as simple as leaving the room when hostilities arise.
- Immediately increase your level of daily exercise. You will feel better physically and emotionally. In addition, an exercise break can create needed personal space and cool down time.

- Find productive, victim free ways to let off steam and vent your frustrations.

Things You Can Do

In addition to helping your family deal with powerlessness and the rising tensions in your household, there are other things you can do to maintain family life while you are unemployed. These actions fall into three categories —Communicate, Establish New Roles and Goals, and Maintain Normality (as much as possible).

Communicate

Consistent open and honest communication is a critical part of helping your family cope with your job loss. Encourage members (with age-group appropriate tasks) to become partners in your reemployment efforts. During your job search, be sure to update your family members weekly without alarming them.

Family members can pat you on the back, act as coaches and cheerleaders, and help you celebrate your accomplishments while you are out of work. However, learn to separate your family life from the job search. The internet allows for 24/7 job hunting and can consume late nights and long weekends. Try not to let the unemployment process "spill" into family time.

Communicate, communicate, communicate . . . but don't assign a family "drill sergeant" to ensure you are job searching. Instead, find a job search buddy.

Encourage family members to share their feelings with you. Your significant other, children, and relatives may want to soften the blow of your unemployment and hide their fears, frustrations, and disappointments. It is your job to gently allay their fears with kindness and sensitivity. Don't let them suffer silently. Do whatever it takes to keep the channels of communication open.

Establish New Roles and Goals

While you are out of work, it is important to redefine your responsibilities, especially in a two-income household family. If your partner is away all day, it might make sense to assume additional household chores. It is helpful and productive to cook dinner, run errands, shop for groceries, pick up the kids, etc.

However, your reemployment efforts must come first. Finding a new job *is* your full-time job. Be sure all family members are clear about their expectations and reassignments of household duties. Don't assume more than your adjusted share of responsibilities out of guilt or shame about being unemployed because this could sabotage your job search.

Maintain Normality

Unemployment affects every aspect of your life—your daily routine, social interactions, steady income, and a host of other things you probably took for granted before being downsized. Now all those things have disappeared along with your job. In the face of all this change, how can your family life go on as before? It won't!

Expect practical changes in your household to accommodate your new financial situation. Try to maintain as much as possible a sense of security. Work hard at protecting the normality of your life.

Don't make any major life decisions—such as moving to a less expensive house or selling your assets. Be proactive in preserving critical aspects of your family's life. Let your lenders, creditors, and utility companies know you've lost your job and negotiate temporary payment plans with them. Stress your intention (in writing) to pay your debts in full as soon as you can. Informing your lenders, in writing, documents your intent and may help protect your credit rating, especially if you are unemployed for a long period of time.

You may be able to negotiate a forbearance agreement with your bank that entitles you to pay interest only on your mortgage until you return to work. Or you may be able to utilize your state's Home Foreclosure Prevention Project.[1]

Once you've taken control of the most important household matters, focus on quality-of-life issues. Your partner, children, and you will become upset if you are afraid to spend money on family activities. But, with a little creativity, you can find low cost/no cost ways of getting out and doing things together. Inquire online or check your local library for free entertainment passes or other local attractions. Look for restaurant specials (during the week) and free concerts, plays, or gallery shows. Check your city's Visitor's Center for brochures about area attractions that may be free. *Focus on abundance, whenever you can, instead of scarcity.*

Keep the romance alive in your marriage while you are unemployed. Consider creating a special dinner for two with a glass of wine by the fireplace once a week. It can give your relationship a well needed boost regardless of how your job search is progressing. If you have young children, ask grandparents, neighbors, or friends to stay with them overnight to allow you a quiet, special time with your partner.

Finally—always remember the vital importance of keeping your reemployment actions separate from family life. Be sure to make time to be a parent, a partner, and a part of the family. When you are finished with the day's job-hunting efforts, turn off your computer and close the door to your office. Leave your job search behind so you can fully participate in whatever is on your family's agenda.

Stop People from Probing into Your Situation

Well-meaning friends and family may feel that it is perfectly appropriate to probe into your job loss. Be prepared for questions and observations that might include phrases like, "Your friend is still employed, so what *really* happened to you," "You didn't deserve this, but this only proves what I've known for some time," "Remember when you told me about the fight you got into with your boss; well, you probably had this coming," "Poor dear, I can't imagine what the neighbors must be saying now," "You've worked for the XYZ company all your life; how will you feed your family?," "I told you not to do such and such, but you wouldn't listen to me—see where it got you, hot shot?," and so on. This is *none* of their business. You need to be prepared for comments like this and understand, in many cases, it is just their way of showing concern.

However, the last thing you need is for others to cross examine you on such a personal and sensitive issue. Prepare ahead with these phrases:

- "I really appreciate your concern, but my full-time job is looking for a full-time job."
- "You may not have read in the paper that the XYZ company laid off *X* number of people, and I was one of those affected by the re-organization."
- "Right now, I am at a crossroads in my career. However, I know I can call on you for help if I need it. . . . Correct?"
- "I'm sure you have a lot of personal connections. Which one of your friends should I be talking to about the ABC industry?"

CHECKLIST

Chapter 2—Secondhand Job Loss

_____   Do family members understand your job loss?

_____   Are small children accepting the cutback of money flow and activities?

_____   Do they understand their new adventure?

_____   Do you need family counseling to help family members cope?

_____   Are you balancing your feelings of scarcity?

_____   Are you communicating and interacting with family and friends (not excluding yourself)?

_____   Is your routine normal—even though your schedule has changed?

_____   Are you working toward a "new" tomorrow?

Life After Unemployment

CHECKLIST

____   Maintain normality—stay in routine with the work day.

____   Understand the Emotional Wave of Unemployment.

____   Outline a career path/track.

____   Obtain additional education and/or training.

____   Develop a unique marketing plan (YOU = BRAND).

____   Develop a job search plan/strategy.

____   Develop 30-second commercial—marketing skills.

____   Develop networking.

____   Understand the types of résumé formats.

____   Develop a mission statement.

____   Create electronic keywords (program search).

____   Emphasize your transferrable skills.

____   DO NOT list personal information.

____   *Proofread . . . proofread . . .* and *proofread* again.
Correct and eliminate typos, errors, and misspellings.

____   Finalize your résumé . . . short, simple, complete.

____   Write a T-square cover letter.

____   Interview—and send thank-you notes.

____   Understand electronic networking protocol.

____   Volunteer in community.

____   Communicate with neighbors, religious leaders, former coworkers.

____   Be persistent—one day at a time.

____   Build momentum through trial and error—small victories/small rewards.

Recovery

At the time of your job loss or downsizing, you will be summoned into your supervisor's office or into a conference room. There, either your supervisor or a representative of the HR department will present you with a folder or a brown business-size envelope prepared by HR. Don't be surprised if your boss is reading from a script. This is usually required by the company to ensure everyone receives the same basic message regarding the company's reason for the downsizing. In most cases, you will be informed that you have up to thirty days to sign and return any documents in the folder. Take your time to read (and reread) carefully at home the literature and any documents. Be sure to cross-check numbers and information against your Employee Hand Book, which usually explains the company's general severance plan.

Company Severance Plans

Typically, when you accept a severance package, you fully and finally release your former employer from any liability for all claims you may have against that employer (regardless of how well documented) in exchange for whatever severance benefits the company is offering to pay you.

If you don't have an employment contract, your employment is likely "at will." This means your employer does not need a good reason to fire you, as long as the motivation is not illegal, as in the cases of discrimination or retaliation. You might hear it referred to as the "hire/fire" law or the "right to work" law, which varies from state to state.[1]

Consider seeking legal advice before you sign your severance agreement, so that you feel confident that you got the best package available. Don't be intimidated by your severance package; try, instead, to negotiate around the company's stated severance formula. If you want something and don't make a counterproposal, you will never know if the company would have accepted your revision. Your former employer may see you as a special case and, therefore, adjust your severance package to include your proposals. Severance packages are always at the option of the company; the longer you hold out signing your severance agreement, the more uncomfortable the company may become. This delay could increase your leverage and negotiating power.

Be sure to request, in writing, a statement that the company will not dispute your unemployment claim. The last time I was unemployed, my former company's corporate HR department disputed my benefits because I was supposedly labeled "incompetent." During the appeal process, I mentioned I had requested from my local boss that the local branch of the company would not dispute my unemployment claim. I provided a copy of an email about my unemployment benefits not being disputed and the controversy was quickly settled. I got full unemployment benefits.

Providing severance packages is a good business practice, but it is not required. Unlike unemployment benefits, severance packages are not mandated by federal law. Here are several items to consider when negotiating your severance package[2]:

- **Income replacement**: This compensation is usually formula based. For example, you may receive a week's salary for every year you have been with the company.
- **Insurance**: Make sure you thoroughly understand your company's policy and how long you will remain qualified for company coverage once your severance period begins and ends. Try to negotiate company-paid healthcare for as long as possible.
- **COBRA**: The Consolidated Omnibus Budget Reconciliation Act of 1986 requires most employers to offer departing employees contin-

ued group health insurance benefits. Brace yourself because once you move from the company's policy to COBRA coverage, you will pay 100 percent of the premiums plus a 2 percent handling fee, dramatically increasing your cost for the same level of healthcare coverage. *Note*: Healthcare may cost less if you join another insurance carrier's group policy. For more information, contact http://www .dol.gov/dol/topic/health-plans/cobra.htm

- **Bonus**: If you are eligible for a bonus, remember to request it, preferably as a lump sum payment.
- **Company email**: Request that the company create an auto-response email message giving your new contact information for a 90-day period.
- **Company voicemail**: Request that the company provide the same information for six-months on voicemail, so people will be able to contact you.
- **Outplacement assistance**: Request outplacement assistance, if not provided.
- **References**: Ensure your former employer will refer all calls regarding your employment to HR. In most cases, the HR department will verify only your inclusive dates of employment. You want to be able to control your references, not your former company.
- **Stocks**: If you are leaving behind unvested stock options, inquire as how long you will be allowed to continue vesting. If no time, request an alternative form of compensation.

Things to Do Immediately

Apply for Unemployment
It is important to apply for unemployment benefits as soon as possible to access the agencies' job-hunting resources, as well as to get your personal information filed in the state's system for other benefits for which you may qualify. In addition, if for any reason your former employer disputes your claim (as in my case above), it will give you time to appeal your case. The

appeal process can last several months depending on circumstances. Here is an overview[3]:

- The Federal–State Unemployment Insurance Program provides benefits to eligible workers who are unemployed through no fault of their own (as determined under state law) and meet other eligibility requirements of state law.
- Unemployment Insurance payments (benefits) are intended to provide temporary financial assistance to unemployed workers who meet requirements of state law.
- Each state administers a separate unemployment insurance program within guidelines established by federal law.
- Eligibility for unemployment insurance and benefits, as well as the length of time your benefits last, are determined by the state law under which unemployment insurance claims are established.
- In the majority of states, benefit funding is based solely on a tax imposed on employers. Three states (Alaska, New Jersey, and Pennsylvania) require minimal employee contributions. Either way, it is important to get the process rolling sooner rather than later.

Mobilize Community Services

To find employment services that may be available in your community, begin by locating your local Career One-Stop Center, which is sponsored by the U.S. Department of Labor, Employment, and Training Administration. Career One-Stop Centers (www.careeronestop.org) are designed to provide information at a local, state, and national level on labor markets and services that use online tools, videos, and maps.[4] Major topics covered include valuable information relative to your job search, such as:

- Exploring new careers
- Salaries and benefits
- Résumés and interviews
- Education and training
- People and places

There are over 2,700 Career One-Stop Centers offering a variety of services throughout the United States. Career One-Stop can have different names in different states. For example, in my home town, the local connection is called the Job Link System, while in Cleveland, Ohio, it is called the Employment Connection. Go to the Career One-Stop website and enter your zip code to find a locator that will pinpoint your closest center.

In addition, there are various levels of services offered, including:

- Comprehensive Career One-Stop Centers provide a full array of employment and training-related services for workers, youth, and businesses. These locations also include staff that can help you with the Workforce Investment Act (WIA).
- Affiliate Career One-Stop Centers provide limited employment and training-related services for workers, youth, and businesses. These locations do not include all on-site agencies funded through the Workforce Investment Act (WIA) (e.g., veterans assistance or vocational rehabilitation).
- Community colleges can provide additional training and/or education (associate degrees, certificates, and diplomas).
- Employment training as funded by the U.S. Department of Labor provides funding for programs to move the workforce investment system in a direction that supports and advances our nation's competiveness.

Remember: These are *your* federal tax dollars at work, so don't be afraid to use them.

Other Community Resources

Many local job search and networking clubs around the country can be very supportive, as well as helpful, in guiding you and increasing your network. A great site with other valuable pieces of job search information is the Riley Guide (http://www.rileyguide.com/support.htm).

You can find more networking and job search support groups in your area by asking at your local public library, local houses of worship (even those you do not attend), college or university career centers, and local OneStopCareer Center. Other community resources to consider may be your local:

- United Way
- Chamber of Commerce
- Council of Governments

Depending on the size of your community, you may need to reach out to similar organizations within a 90-mile radius of your home.

What *NOT* to Do and Why

- **Do not immediately put your house up for sale.** Your home is the single largest asset you own. *Be careful.* Francis, a member of Professionals in Transition® Support Group Inc. (PIT®), lost her job and thought nothing of putting her house on the market while she began her job search. Her house sold after the first open house. Francis was forced to leave her home and move in with her mother, living three hours away in another state. Three months later (you guessed it), Francis got a job offer from a company less than 30 minutes from the home she had just recently sold.
- **Don't flame your old company** regardless of how you feel and no matter how badly you have been treated. Remember, a potential employer is looking for what you can do in the future. If you kill your career karma (reputation) by blasting your old company, it will create a negative impression of you. Take the high road—it can pay off for you later because what goes around comes around.
- **Be careful what you say in public** about former employees and previous employers; the person you're talking to could be a friend, golf buddy, neighbor, fellow church member, or relation of a key person in your old company. Your toxic words will get back to your former company, and people tend to have "elephant-like" memories. You have to decide on your own code of conduct, but remember that retaliation will never serve you well.

- **Fight the urge to send out an old résumé.** Take time to effectively market who you are on paper. Know where you want to go next. Flooding the market with an old résumé will only confuse companies that receive them and the people who read them.

- **Do not send a sloppy email to anyone** (regardless of how well you know them). Often, families and friends want to help you, sometimes in ways you cannot plan or predict. They could easily forward what was meant to be a personal and confidential email to a potential employer without telling you because they don't want to get your hopes up. An angry, critical, negative, sloppy, poorly constructed, or misspelled email can quickly become an embarrassment and restrict your progress.

- **Don't spend all of your days at home applying for jobs listed on the Internet.** Get away from your computer and out into the community. Less than 7 percent of all jobs come from the Internet. By that I mean: someone saw the position on the Internet, applied for the position online, negotiated for the position, and got the job. This 7 percent plus another 13 percent that comes from all other visible job sources (e.g., newspapers, trade magazines, job fairs) is where the vast majority of people search for jobs. More than 80 percent of jobs are found through networking. Networking will be discussed in greater detail in Step Five: "The Power of Networking."

- **Finally, do not keep your job loss and job search a secret.** This is much easier said than done. Losing your job is embarrassing, and it is human nature not to want to tell friends or neighbors because they may look at you differently. You may feel that not having a job "looks bad" or wonder "how can they possibly help, they don't work in my field." By keeping your job loss a secret you are starving yourself of potential networking connections and may be missing many job leads that will never appear in the paper or online. One of my mentors, Dr. Nido Qubein, President of High Point University, once told me the secret to life is to "stand tall and be proud." Job loss is a humbling experience. Asking for help can be hard, but if you don't, you definitely won't receive the invaluable help, guidance, or support critical to reemployment. Stand tall and be proud. Job loss is what it is, and you will rise above it. Regardless of the circumstances, you can control your career direction into the future.

CHECKLIST

Chapter 3—Recovery

_____   Do you understand your severance package?

_____   If not, have you contacted someone from the company for a better understanding of your benefits?

_____   Do you need legal assistance?

_____   Do you understand your state's labor laws?

_____   Have you applied for unemployment benefits?

_____   Have you researched available community services at your city's Department of Employment Security or local library?

_____   Do you know what to do and what not to do?

Getting Organized

Job loss is chaotic and will become overwhelming *unless* you are organized. A recent poll on SimplyHired.com found a third of job seekers consider themselves "very organized" and a quarter "extremely organized." However, 27 percent of job seekers said they were only slightly organized, while 13 percent said they were not organized at all. Staying organized keeps you focused on your search and helps to keep track of your progress.[1]

Easy Ways to Organize Your Job Search

A little organization can go a long way when it comes to managing the process of finding a new job. An organized job search will be more time effective and efficient. It will allow you to stay on top of the process and easily find critical files and contacts. Getting organized does not have to be a complex process. Simple ways to get organized include the following.

Efficient Office Space

To effectively job search, you will need a dedicated space. A separate room free of traffic is your best bet. If that's not possible, get creative. You may need to rearrange furniture—move a bookshelf, desk, or other large piece of furniture to divide a room—and use the quieter half as an office. Ask family members to respect your work space and time spent job searching. Close the door if you have one.

Once you have established a work area, equip your "office" with materials you will need to conduct your job search. If you plan to use a home phone, be sure to change your voice message to a business style (same thing with a personal cell phone). One of the quickest ways to alienate a potential job opportunity is to have a voicemail that is cute instead of professional. HR managers have told me they either hang up or question if they have called the right telephone number when they hear a "cutesy" voice response. Be enthusiastic in your voice message to avoid sounding depressed.

Establishing a Daily Routine

Your full-time job is now searching for a full-time job. To create job search momentum, you need to be searching a minimum of five hours a day/five days a week. The working world goes on with or without you. Be sure to stay "in sync" with the business day according to its usual schedule. Even though you no longer have a schedule to follow or a boss to answer to, you must follow a daily routine and *be accountable to yourself.* Set your alarm to ensure you are "up and at it" with a defined plan of attack. Avoid the tendency to continually stay up late and sleep in. A daily routine creates structure and keeps you connected with the working world. It will provide comfort and allow you to work nine to five, instead of being a 24/7 job searcher. It reinforces your daily commitment to find a job. A regular daily routine will allow you to move forward and stay positive.

Chunking

But how do you begin? Start by reviewing your goals for the day. Break your day into small, manageable increments or chunks of time so that:

- You might spend your first hours searching for positions.
- Once you have identified potential jobs, fill out job applications— one by one.
- From there, you might follow up with telephone calls, emails, and other means of correspondence.

The key is taking *small steps daily,* gradually building momentum that eventual leads to interviews and, ultimately, a job. Chunking time reduces the chances you will become paralyzed or intimidated by the job search process.

Keeping a Calendar and/or Schedule

You can easily lose track of daily goals, weekly outcomes, upcoming interviews, appointments, or scheduled follow-ups with employers without the help of a calendar or day planner. Many electronic calendars can be set to notify you a certain amount of time before an upcoming event so you can prepare in advance. Your calendar (and reminders) can be on your computer, your phone, or a written, daily planner. It is important to use whatever means you are most comfortable and familiar using.

Finding Contacts

Regardless of whether you use an address book, notebook, card file, or software database, it is critical that you be able to find information quickly. Now is the time to build your database of contacts. Consider people with whom you have worked and add individuals you may know from the community, your health club, school or your children's school, church, or volunteer activities.

Manage your contacts by keeping track of how you met them, who introduced you, and their contact information (physical home and email addresses, business and mobile telephone numbers, and company physical and email addresses). This may serve you later as a reference list when you need recommendations and/or references.

Managing Correspondence

As you begin to send out cover letters and résumés for various job opportunities, you will find yourself with multiple versions of cover letters, résumés, thank-you notes (and a job search spreadsheet if you are required to track your job applications while collecting unemployment compensation). You can become confused. To avoid confusion, track all your correspondence. Organization creates a feeling of control and confidence as you begin your job search campaign.

Create folders (on your computer) using a naming strategy that makes sense to you. Consider generic file names such as:

- Companies
- Résumés
- Cover letters
- Thank-you notes
- Job search spreadsheet

Within each file, name or identify your document(s) accordingly, such as:

- Company name—position
- Company name—addressee's name

Use some identifier that will indicate how application/correspondence was made to a particular company. Your computer system will automatically date your correspondence once you have saved your document.

Always back up your job search efforts to a separate memory stick or flash drive. Name your memory stick something identifiable (like employment). It is easily carried with you in the event you need information relative to an application, job history, contact list, etc.

Another option is to use online services, such as Carbonite or Google Drop Box. These services allow you to back up your files in the "cloud."

Organizing Your Email

Avoid any chance of losing critical information by creating an individual mail folder for your work search correspondence. Within the folder, create subfolders (as needed) by company. This way you avoid losing any email with important information as your job search process moves forward.

Creating a Job Search Record

It is important to track and update your progress. One of the best ways is to create a job search record in Excel or set up a table in Word (see Exhibit 4-1). This document allows you to stay in control of your job search and quickly keep track of the status of all your job applications. Record each position you've applied for making note of the following information:

- Date
- Company
- Contact information (i.e., telephone number, email address)
- Job posting location (i.e., web address, newspaper, etc.)
- Job title
- Current status (follow ups, results, comments, thank-you notes)
- Next steps

Exhibit 4-1   Job Search Record

DATE OF CONTACT	EMPLOYER'S NAME	EMPLOYER'S ADDRESS	EMAIL ADDRESS	TELEPHONE NUMBER	TYPE OF WORK	RESULT
8/27/2013	The Budd Group	WS, NC			Exec Assist	
8/22/2013	Guilford Co. Schools	GSO, NC			Exec Assist I	
8/21/2013	PepsiCo	WS, NC			Admin Asst Re# 17287BR	
8/17/2013	Fairview UMC	Pinnacle, NC			Church Secretary	
8/17/2013	Ajilon Prof Staffing	WS, NC			Exec Assist US_EN_7-20744-33756683	
8/13/2013	Moravian Church in America	WS, NC			Exec Assist	
8/10/2013	Wake Forest (WFU)	WS, NC			Admin Coord #978-141	
8/8/2013	B/E Aerospace	WS, NC			Admin Assist 10188	

Note: This type of record is also required by most state employment offices as verification of job search efforts.

As you continue your job search, update your spreadsheet, particularly if you find or talk to a decision maker or someone involved with a potential job. Add columns to reflect specific information (e.g., follow-up dates, interview dates, thank-you notes sent, etc.).

Increase your focus on active job leads by crossing out jobs (or cutting and pasting them to another spreadsheet, entitled "Inactive") when you learn they have been filled or you are no longer being considered for the position. By continuing to update this form, you will remain on task instead of wasting time on positions already filled. It is important to remember that employers can take weeks—sometimes months—to get back to you, so allow time for several attempts to contact them before crossing that potential job off your list.

Another benefit of your spreadsheet is following potential industry hiring trends. Your records will reveal valuable information, such as how long it typically takes specific employers to respond. If you know you're searching for work in an industry that typically offers employment two months after the original application, you'll have a greater ability to estimate the length of time it will take for a company to complete the hiring process and, therefore, to determine whether you should continue pursuing this position or move on to another.

Tracking your applications will also show who is responding and if certain types of employers are more receptive to your résumé than others. For instance, you may notice a trend in that large corporations do not respond to your résumé. This might be a sign that your résumé is not standing out to that type of employer.

Job Search Expenses

A computer and printer are critical job search tools. If you do not have a computer or printer, you may be able to purchase one and take the expense as a tax deduction in your job search.

In addition, office supplies (including computer ink and paper), Internet service, mobile phone expense (if this is your sole source of communication), newspaper subscriptions, trade journals, self-help books, professional résumé writing services, career counseling, schooling, memberships, travel time and mileage (documented with receipts) to and from job interviews and/or schooling, along with anything else used to search for a job or assist you in getting a job may be considered tax deductible. This also applies to new clothes you may need for a job interview. *Be sure to consult the Internal Revenue Service for current deductions or consult with your tax planner for further guidance.*

CHECKLIST

Chapter 4—Getting Organized

____   Have you established a defined workspace?

____   Have you started pulling together a functional office with supplies?

____   Are you reviewing your goals daily?

____   Are you maintaining a business schedule/hours?

____   Are you chunking your time effectively?

____   Does your family understand your new work schedule?

____   Have you organized your contacts?

____   Have you established a system for keeping up with "job search" expenses?

____   Are you building your Job Search Record and following the Job Search checklist?

____   Have you established an email filing system to track correspondence?

5

Rebuilding Your Professional Identity

Your income, future, lifestyle, and security have been *yanked out from under you* by your former company without your permission. Regardless of your age or life experience, job elimination forces you to involuntarily give up the professional identity, reputation, and work life you have achieved. This sudden change makes hiding your emotions almost impossible and reluctantly forces you to adjust to a new way of living.

Job loss can easily be viewed as a personal attack on your expertise, knowledge, abilities, and level of contribution. Today's workforce centers on working in teams. Now that you no longer have a company or team to work for, it is common to feel left behind, betrayed, and disappointed. You built strong relationships with the people on your team and developed further support across a broad circle of work acquaintances. Sharing that camaraderie with former workmates will soon come to an end because you are now considered an "outsider" looking in. You quickly find out who your true friends are and who your work acquaintances were.

Getting Back in Balance

Rebuilding your identity (both professional and personal) is about returning to a state of equilibrium. This is accomplished by reconstructing a new self-image, a new lifestyle, and even a new professional uniqueness. The need to abandon what previously defined your professional life can be agonizing.

But, if you do not let go and embrace the future, potential opportunities may pass you by. Gradually, as you accept the present situation, you will begin to feel a new anticipation and excitement toward the future.

Your job search experience is unique to yourself—your needs, experiences, and insights are unlike those of others and are exclusive in their own way. Steps to rebuilding your personal identity include the following.

Reestablishing Personal Control

In most cases you probably had absolutely no control over the elimination of your job. Sometimes (particularly if you had a personality conflict with your boss), you may have contributed to your job loss. Regardless of the reasons, reestablishing personal control is the first step toward marketing yourself—preparing yourself mentally and moving forward. The next step is to recognize you have control over what happens.

Take control of life by maintaining your daily routine (See Chapter 4, "Getting Organized"). Establishing and maintaining a daily routine provides structure and predictability. You know every day that you're doing everything possible to find a job. This knowledge allows you to take control of your life and actions.

Your daily commitment to following the job search process will create momentum toward getting that next opportunity. Each day will reinforce that your full-time job is finding a full-time job. Job searching eight hours a day sounds like a lot of time, but that time should include attendance at networking events, community events, volunteer activities, and attendance at least one support group. Eight hours of concentrated work allows you to end each day feeling good about your efforts and allows you to transition from job searching to your regular role of partner, parent, or any other role you might have.

Going Easy on Yourself

It's natural to beat yourself up for your job loss. The guilt and shame can be overwhelming. Respect the fact that you are in your most vulnerable and weakest state, but realize that you are a strong individual who will recuperate over time.

Be prepared for the endless thoughts and questions that pour into your mind about your past and present circumstances. Understand that you may be temporarily overwhelmed when thinking about your future. When it comes to job loss—*it is what it is.* No matter how difficult it is, the only way out is by taking back control of your thoughts. Earl Nightingale, a motivational speaker, once said "We become what we think about." and that "attitude is everything."[1]

Preserving Your Weekends

Avoid becoming a 24/7 job searcher. Instead, walk away from your computer and into the weekend without guilt. Consider maintaining your regular weekend routine. Mow the lawn, putter around your garden, do other small projects, pursue your hobbies, or do anything else you enjoy doing on weekends.

Will you miss potentially good jobs if you take weekends off? No. In most cases, job opportunities are listed for at least six days. Here's why. If you have been diligent in your job search routine, you have covered all jobs (on the Internet) that have appeared throughout the week. On Monday (with your first initial swoop of the day), you will pick up any job positions that may have been posted over the weekend.

Allowing 48 to 72 hours downtime allows you to decompress and relax. The free time enables you to clear your mind, enjoy your family and friends, and spend time on hobbies or just enjoying Mother Nature. Walk in the park. Take a drive to the beach. Play sports. Go to a party. Attend the religious institution of your faith. New surroundings offer a different group of people to socialize and/or network with (see Chapter 17, "Social Networking"). On Monday morning, you will emerge refreshed and ready to go to work again—job searching.

Coordinating and Aligning Your Thoughts

As you begin to move forward and start to process your job loss, be open to new experiences. Now is the time to explore your dreams and think outside of the box. Moving on is difficult because you are leaving behind a comfortable old professional identity and starting on a new you.

Moving forward you will need to channel your thoughts, feelings, and actions into a positive attitude. You have to believe in yourself before others will believe in you. If you don't believe in yourself, you will have a difficult time finding the momentum to feel motivated to creating a new you. You must gather the strength from within to be positive. Being positive throughout the job search process is crucial, because no employer wants to hire a negative employee. Staying positive, however, is *easier said than done*, because job searching is a long and lonely process. You will experience many low points of no luck, no interviews, and no prospects. There will be high points of hope centered on what appears to be plenty of job opportunities. During the low points of your job search, you may question yourself and your self-esteem will waiver. So *thinking positively*, no matter how difficult things may be, is a critical attribute you need to keep in the forefront of your persona.

Improving Your Attitude

To improve your attitude you might consider listening to motivational specialists, including Earl Nightingale, Zig Ziglar, Dale Carnegie, Tony Robbins, Nido Quebein, and Napoleon Hill. These experts provide guidance for making genuine changes in the way you look at the world and at your job search. They offer help, encouragement, and hope during the long and solitary days of job searching. These various speakers were very helpful to me during the several times I was out of work. Their perspectives were each a little different, but their messages and beliefs provided me with comfort, direction, and perspective.

Managing Ongoing Stress

There is a high probability that you will experience overwhelming amounts of stress. It is important to review what stress does and does not do[2]:

- Stress *does* erode your perception of the situation at hand.
- Stress *does* contribute to feelings of helplessness and lack of control.
- Stress *does* contribute to feelings of self-pity regarding job loss.
- Stress *does not* improve your chances of getting a new job, mastering new skills, or getting out of a rut.

- Stress *does not* help you maintain existing relationships that are impacted by the loss of your job, including those with friends, family, and others who depend on you.

Managing Shame

Sometimes you will be overwhelmed with shame-provoked, job loss related thoughts. It may take the form of stomach cramps, headache, or in the tightening of your solar plexus. Perhaps your face will burn as you blush. Remember, though, that confronting shame is a natural byproduct of job loss. Your professional identity and dignity has been stripped without your plan or permission.

Millions of people who have been unemployed before you have felt the same way. You are not alone in feeling shame; I did when I was out of work.

Here are a few things you can do[3]:

- Fight feelings of shame with balanced, positive, tangible thoughts about yourself.
- Understand that unemployment is temporary and that there is a job out there with your name on it.
- Reach out to others less fortunate than you. By helping others, you will truly help yourself. It will change your perspective and restore your self-worth. You will realize that there is nothing to be ashamed of and that others need and appreciate your service and talents.
- When overwhelmed with the shame and sadness of my job loss, I found myself returning to some of the critical life tips I learned at Al-Anon that included: "Let go and let God" and live life "One Day at a Time." When starting Professionals In Transition® Support Group Inc. (PIT®), I was looking for an "Al-Anon for the unemployed." Because there was nothing like that anywhere in the country, I started PIT®.

Maintaining Professional Relationships

Job loss can crush professional relationships. You may be confused as to whether you should try to stay in touch with former colleagues—or even if it would be appropriate. You may find that when you try to contact them at work, conversations are awkward. If they seem uncomfortable when they return your call, ask them if there is a better time or alternative phone number on which you can call them. This is the work acquaintances versus true friend indicator test. If they encourage you to call back at a better time or provide an alternative number, they have passed the test.

If your calls go unreturned or if they don't provide an alternative time or number, they just flunked the test. Sadly, in many cases, people you think are most likely to pass will flunk. Those who flunk your test may make you feel as if you have the unemployment plague.

The truth is that transitions are a natural part of life. Understand these are life events that we all go through. However, life events feel different to everyone. You must not hide from this involuntary and, often, untimely change. Instead of avoiding people, reach out to them. They may be afraid to contact you because they don't know what to say. Accept their words of empathy and support. Let them know that you may need their help in the future.

Nourish your social contacts. You might consider hosting a potluck dinner to bring your friends and supporters around. Promise that nothing about work will be discussed. This will help minimize your sense of loss and everyone's stress levels. Or, as mentioned earlier, consider volunteering. Not only will you realize that you have much more to give than what the job loss took, you will meet interesting people who may be able to help you network.

Giving Yourself Plenty of Time

Rebuilding your personal and professional identities takes time. Rushing prematurely into new activities, experiences, and even jobs may only encourage the repetition of old habits and feelings. Instead, learn to:

- Slow down.
- Tackle your "to-do" list.
- Work on hobbies or other tasks that bring you happiness and help to create a feeling of confidence.

All of these will allow you to feel productive and provide comfort while you manage job transition and changes brought about because of unemployment.

Indulge yourself during this transition, and find the support you need (including, if appropriate, a professional therapist who can provide you with guidance through your transition). Do not try to escape or avoid your situation, but continue to face and challenge it. Challenge yourself. Most importantly *trust* yourself, because you will overcome unemployment and then begin the next life transition into a new job.

CHECKLIST

Chapter 5—Rebuilding Your Professional Identity

_____ Do you need to communicate with professionals who can help you cope with the reality of your job loss?

_____ Have you accepted your job loss as a situation out of your control?

_____ Do you understand you can only change what is current?

_____ Are you managing reality?

_____ Are you communicating with family and friends who care about you?

_____ Are you acknowledging the wave of various emotions associated with the sudden loss of professional identity?

_____ Are you allowing yourself enough time to pull it together to start a new stage in your life?

Developing a Career Plan

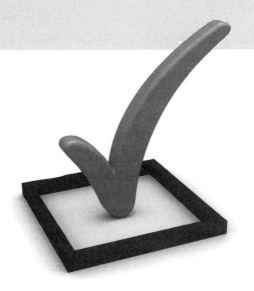

CHECKLIST

_____   Outline a career path/track.

_____   Test yourself: Online Professional Personality Test

      _____   Know your transferrable skills.

_____   Obtain education and/or training for new career path.

_____   Develop a unique marketing plan.

      _____   Market your differential advantages.

      _____   Résumé, cover letter, business cards.

_____   Develop a job search plan/strategy.

_____   Practice marketing skills (sell yourself to yourself).

      _____   30-second commercial.

_____   Develop networking skills one person at a time.

_____   Continue to "feed and nourish" list of references.

_____   Maintain normality.

      _____   Exercise.

      _____   Interact with friends and family.

      _____   Maintain a positive attitude.

6

Developing Your Career Plan

There's no magic in looking for a job. It all comes down to developing an effective plan for reemployment. As you have already experienced, a job search is hard work. Creating a plan requires taking an honest look at yourself and asking key questions about your strengths, weaknesses, likes, and dislikes. The following steps will guide you in the process of creating an effective job search plan.

Creating a Job Search Plan

Looking Back to Look Ahead

Take the first step toward building your future by looking back. No work experience, regardless of how painful it may have been, was in vain. Throughout your career you learned what you were capable of doing, what you enjoyed doing, and what you hated doing but needed to do to get the job done. Now that you have a built-in distance from your last job, take a look at your work experience through a different looking glass. Here is a starter list of questions to ask yourself:

- What did I like best/least about my last job?
- What were my most important and satisfying accomplishments?
- What did I like best/least about the company?
- What did I like best/least about the people for whom I worked?
- What were my most significant failures?
- What kind of negative feedback did I receive?

- What was missing from my last job that I want to seek in a new position?

Ask these same questions about other positions (including volunteer jobs) you've held. By honestly answering questions similar to those above, you are taking the first step toward achieving personal awareness and professional success.

Comparing Work Experiences

Compare yourself at different stages of your work experience:

- In which job(s) were you happiest? Why?
- In which job(s) were you most successful? Why?
- What management style was the best/worst you ever experienced? Why?
- Has your career growth been stunted by any barriers?
- If you could start your career over again, what would you do differently?

Finding Your Transferable Skills

Transferrable skills are abilities you enjoy doing and do well. They are natural talents and core abilities (often learned from life's experiences). To pinpoint these skills, it is important for you to identify at least twenty accomplishments from all times of your life: school, work (from your early career to the present), volunteer activities, hobbies, etc. It doesn't matter how old you were or what other people thought, nor does it matter if you got paid. Events from childhood can be important because they took place when you were not trying to please a boss. The more important values are how you felt when you completed the task and that you could easily see a tangible benefit.

Capture your accomplishments in writing. Describe the situation in as much detail as possible. Relative to your accomplishments, ask questions like:

- What was the purpose or goal?
- What did you do (step by step)?

- How long did it last?
- What was the outcome?

Share your stories (of accomplishments) with a family member or friend. Ask them if they remember when you did it, and invite them to share their impression of the incident. They may be able to provide valuable feedback and help you remember other times you performed a similar task. Once you've gathered your twenty accomplishments, rank them by importance and distill the list down to the top seven stories.

The Enjoyable Accomplishment Approach (or "Seven Stories Approach") is used by many outplacement organizations. Bernard Haldane is credited with creating the outplacement method of having clients recall stories about satisfying accomplishments, concentrating on those they achieved without effort and enjoyed immensely. Haldane (and those who followed in his footsteps) then had clients choose the most significant stories (or experiences), thus creating a concept called "dependable strengths."[4]

Marketing Other Transferable Skills

If you're like most people, you live for more than just work. Many times the things you most enjoy doing and from which you receive the greatest level of gratification are not work related. Look to your leisure activities for transferable skills. Perhaps you have instructed others, written, coached, collected, analyzed, programmed, or managed. The knowledge you've gained and the skills you've picked up while outside the workplace might help to validate a different skill set required in a different career or add increased knowledge/value to an old one.

Finding the Professional You

Understanding your core skills helps validate your working life and creates a sense of personal stability. Knowing your strengths gives you flexibility and allows you to build on an established career path or may encourage you to explore a new avenue toward employment satisfaction. You will worry less about mistakes in the past; instead, you look at them as learning opportunities.

Determining your reliable skills is the first step in career planning. Identifying past successes, current strengths, and personal preferences is an enormous step toward rebuilding you and your self-presentation.

It's easy to lose your confidence and perspective when you've recently been terminated. But losing a job doesn't make you any less of a person. It simply presents a challenge to overcome. Take the opportunity to ask yourself these questions:

- How do I typically react to extreme stress and pressure?
- What has been the most difficult kind(s) of work problems I have had to handle?
- How do I typically react when 1 am being criticized?
- What are some of the rewards I expect from work?
- What are my short-range and long-term career objectives?
- Have I ruled out any career alternatives I should now reconsider?

What's Your Dream Job?

If you could indulge your hobbies and interests by turning them into a money-making venture, would you? Close your eyes for a few minutes, and see yourself engaged in your dream job. Alternatively, imagine doing what you like best or something you've done in the past that's given you incredible satisfaction. Visualize (down to the smallest details) your environment, the people and objects around you, and what you're doing.

Use all your senses. Hear the sounds, feel the textures, smell the aromas, and taste the tastes. Imagine it's happening now and take the time to fully experience it. Then open your eyes, while holding the image, and consider:

- What are the most appealing aspects of your fantasy?
- What are the most realistic aspects?
- What are the most absurd?
- What goals would you have to achieve to make your fantasy come true?
- What are the barriers to achieving those goals?
- How can you overcome them?

Even if you've worked in the same industry throughout your career, you don't have to stay in it for the duration. There's no reason to feel stuck or to continue pursuing a career in a field that no longer interest you. Before you commit to a job, do your homework—target industries where you would like to work, where you would be the "right fit." Since you're in search mode, be more objective than you were in the past about what you want to do next. Depending on your expertise and/or education, it might be a relatively simple transfer of skills and interests from one industry to another.

Survey Your Field

Ultimately you will gain a "reality check" in your field surveys and career direction by means of informational interviewing. But before you discover the hidden job market through informational interviewing, continue reading trade magazines, industry newsletters, and local and national business newspapers. Attend trade shows and association meetings. Assess the current state of your industry and the changes that are happening. Begin with the following questions:

- How do industry experts rate the field's health today?
- What major changes are being predicted for the field?
- What factors will help the industry during the next decade?
- What are the biggest threats the industry will face in the next decade?
- In what geographical areas will the field be the strongest?
- What types of people and skills will be in the greatest demand?
- What advantages and disadvantages to working in the field currently loom largest?

In addition, consider asking:

- With the skills you have now, are you and the field still a good match?
- Are there additional classes you must take to achieve longevity in the industry?
- Over the long haul, would the industry be able to pay you enough to meet your financial needs?
- Would you be able to stay close to home for the foreseeable future if you stayed in your field? If not, would you and your family be

willing to relocate to the geographical areas where the industry is growing?

- Are there other industries to which you could transfer your job skills and interests?
- Would any of these be a better match for you?

Arm yourself with all of the information you need to help you decide if a change of direction makes sense for you.

Your Personal Career Plan

Writing a career plan creates personal direction and focus. A written personal career plan is a tangible and measurable outcome and serves as a roadmap to job search success. Now that you've given some thought to your career plans and conducted research into the economic realities, do the following exercise:

- Write down ten industry and job description options and rank them from 1–10.
- Decide on the three best alternatives to your current course.
- Identify the action steps you'll have to take to pursue them.

Create a Career Summary

You've taken steps toward assessing your work and life experiences and contemplated where you would best fit in the workplace. Now it's time to design your career summary, to showcase you at your highest level of effectiveness. A good script for developing a career summary begins by filling in the following:

- Industry
- Title
- Areas of experience (packed with key words relative to the industry)

Several samples are shown below:

- "Finance Director with extensive experience in financial planning and budgeting, variance analysis, financial reporting, operational, compliance, and financial auditing. An effective leader and communicator, with strong business mindset. Strengths include data analysis, process improvements, and customer relations."

- "Senior Business Manager with progressive operational, customer service, accounting, finance, and administrative experience. A results-oriented team player with proven leadership, management, process, negotiation, and organizational skills, combined with strong operational, analytical, financial, procedural, and technical abilities."

- "Versatile professional with extensive experience in manufacturing, product development, and process improvement. Able to perform in a fast-paced, quality-driven, team-based manufacturing environment. Proficient in delivering cost-effective solutions to meet customer needs."

Don't let the samples above intimidate you. We will discuss more about developing your Career Summary in Chapter 9, "Personal Marketing Plan," and Chapter 10, "Résumé Components."

Remember that a career summary sets forth your "dependable strengths" and transferrable skills. These may change during the course of your job search. For that reason, you may want to reevaluate your career summary.

CHECKLIST

Chapter 6—Developing Your Career Plan

Have you listed:

____   Work history?

____   Current skill set?

____   Immediate job-ready skills needing to be learned (e.g., Internet, email, job aggregators, LinkedIn, Skpe, Word, Excel, PowerPoint, Access, etc.)?

____   Next steps?

____   Current demand for the skill set?

____   Local, state, and government career counseling resources?

____   Available funding for retraining or additional schooling?

7

All-Important Research

It takes time to research a company or a job opportunity. But if you don't do your research thoroughly, you won't have the critical information needed to make good decisions. Finding the right job is an investment in your future. There is nothing worse or more time consuming than having to start all over again because the job didn't work out.

Many research options are available to help you find key information about particular industries, companies, decision makers, and job openings. Although multiple research channels exist, you must determine which ones give you the greatest return for your time spent.

In-Person Networking

- Conducting face-to-face networking through informational interviews
- Attending professional association meetings
- Joining job search support groups
- Attending college alumni get-togethers
- Participating in Chambers of Commerce events
- Going to job fairs
- Attending any other in-person event where you gather information about potential openings and target companies

Matt Youngquist, the president of Career Horizons, tells job seekers that most job hunters (still) "are spending 70 or 80 percent of their time surfing the net versus getting out there, talking to employers," taking chances [and] realizing that the vast majority of hiring is friends and acquaintances hiring other trusted friends and acquaintances."[1]

Local Resources

Local resources include your closest unemployment office or any other community or church-based job search location. Your local library is a great resource for access to the Internet, hardbound business journals, directories, magazines, newspapers, and other specialized publications, including:

- Hoover's Master List of Major U.S. Corporations (www.hoovers.com)
- Electronic databases, including EDGAR (which stands for Electronic Data Gathering, Analysis, and Retrieval), help you with real-time information on all foreign and domestic companies that are required to file registration statements, periodic reports, and other forms filed electronically through the EDGAR system for the U.S. Securities and Exchange Commission. (SEC). (http://www.sec.gov/edgar/aboutedgar.htm)
- Business Dateline provides the full text of major news and feature stories from 550 regional business publications from throughout the United States and Canada (http://library.dialog.com/bluesheets/html/bl0635.html)

Basic Internet Resources

The Internet is one of the most powerful tools for finding career opportunities and retrieving information on specific companies and industry trends. The data that you receive is dynamic, up-to-date, and reflects current world perspective. Don't be like the poor job search candidate who failed to check the company's website the day of his big interview. Dated information about a critical new company product release eliminated his prospects with the company minutes into the interview.

If you are changing careers and don't know where to begin, the Occupational Information Network (O*NET) is a great source available through the U.S. Department of Labor/Employment and Training Administration (USDOL/ETA). The O*NET program is the nation's primary source of occupational information (www.onetcenter.org). The database contains information on hundreds of standardized and occupation-specific job descriptions that allow users to find occupations to explore, match skill sets, review related occupations, and connect with other online resources.

The number of websites can be overwhelming, so find your favorites and allocate your time accordingly. Although many of these sites are not research related, the sheer number of possibilities can be a major source of distraction while job searching. A March 2012 Netcraft discovered 644,275,754 active websites.[2] Limit your time instead only to job-search related websites, including:

- Your target list of companies websites.
- Search Engines, such as Google and Yahoo.
- Job aggregators, such as Indeed.com and SimplyHired.com.
- Social networking sites, such as Facebook, Twitter, and MySpace.
- Free databases, such as www.CrunchBase.com, which lists technology companies, or www.FindArticles.com, which provides full-text articles.
- The *Book of Lists,* which is available yearly from www.bizjournals .com.
- Magazines, such as *Fortune, Inc., Business Week, Fast Company,* and *Forbes,* which feature specific companies. Every spring *Fortune* magazine publishes its directory of the 500 largest industrial corporations and the top 1,000 companies.
- *The Wall Street Journal* (www.wsj.com) *and The Wall Street Journal Index, as* well as *Barron's,* yearly listing in alphabetical order of articles appearing in *The Wall Street Journal.*

Be sure to balance your time between networking and online job searching.

Trade/Professional Newsletters and Journals

Read your industry's trade journals to identify key sources for jobs, contacts, and changes in your field. Any change described could be a possible lead for you. If someone is promoted or a new product is introduced, this information could prompt you to call with congratulations or to see a new need for your expertise and provide a reason to network, contact, and meet.

Company Blogs

Company blogs provide a voice for a company that educates and informs website visitors. They are often supported by the company and tell potential employees about the company's culture. There are also blogs written by employees and former employees. You can gain valuable insights into the issues a company is promoting by reading its blog. However, blogs written by former employees usually discuss the hidden underbelly of the organization—the issues the company does not want discussed in public.

Online Career Networking

Sites like LinkedIn, Monster, Bright Star, and a variety of other online career networking websites can help you get in touch with networkers at specific companies, with college groups, or with companies in targeted geographical areas. In addition, if you're a college graduate, your institution may have an alumni career network you can access.

Join a Discussion Group

Vault's company specific message boards will help you get the inside scoop on career fields and employers that interest you. You will be able to research a specific job or the company hiring process. For example, if you were considering a career change to financial planning, you may be able to find a discussion on what you can expect to be paid as a financial adviser, what type of background check will be conducted if you're offered the job, and a variety of other topics relevant to employment with the company.

Professional Associations

If you belong to a professional association, attend a meeting or check the website to see what networking opportunities are available. If you aren't a current member, consider joining a professional association in your field. Research what information and/or services they can provide you before you join.

Read, Read, and Read

If you're interested in employment close to home, local business newspapers and the business section of your local newspaper are an ideal way to keep up to date on local happenings. Information on new companies and updates on local businesses are published there on a regular basis, as well as on company websites. Set up news alerts for companies in which you are particularly interested.

It takes time to research a company or a job opportunity. But if you don't do your research thoroughly, you won't have the critical information you need to make a good decision. Finding the right job is an investment in your future.

CHECKLIST

Chapter 7—All-Important Research

_____   Did you know that 80 percent of jobs are found through networking?
_____   Did you know that 80 percent of job openings are *not* published?
_____   Did you know that most hard-copy data is also available online?
_____   Are you properly balancing your time between networking and online researching?

In addition, are you:
_____   Reading trade and/or professional newsletters and journals?
_____   Networking as a member of a professional association?
_____   Using online career networking sites?
_____   Reading company blogs?
_____   Tracking targeted companies by means of LinkedIn and social networking sites?

8

Personality Testing

Employers do not like to make mistakes when hiring new employees. In addition to your résumé, work history, experience, education, and performance skills, personality testing continues to grow as a part of the hiring process. Standardized personality tests allow employers to predict your cultural fit and potential success (as it applies to the job you applied for). In many cases, you will find a mandatory personality test must be completed before your online application is accepted.

A poll conducted by the Society for Human Resource Management showed that more than 23 percent of surveyed organizations used "online minimum qualification screening questionnaires—questions that may knock candidates out of the recruiting process."[1]

Experts estimate that pre-hire testing of potential employees has grown as much as 20% annually and high turnover industries like retail, hospitality, and food service use these tests the most.[2]

Personality tests are legal, but the law is different in every state. As long as the test meets professional standards, it can be a mandatory part of the application process. In addition, no laws entitle the job seeker to view the results of the test.[3]

I discovered this firsthand when I applied for a position with a national department store chain. In addition to having six interviews in six hours, I was sent to a psychologist's office for personality testing and conversation. I was astonished when I found out that results of this test were the property of the chain and that the results would not be shared with me.

Although you can always refuse to take a personality test, you do so at your own risk. You may never be told you didn't get the job because of this decision, but keep in mind that your refusal could raise an automatic "flag" and become a barrier to being hired or moving forward within the company (if hired).

The Most Common Personality Tests

You will most likely encounter one of three tests during the hiring process. Many of these tests have been verified over the life of the personality instrument. For more information, go to https://cdn.theladders.net/static/images/editorial/weekly/pdfs/personality-job-search.pdf

The 16 PF (16 Personality Factor Questionnaire)

This test measures 16 normal-range personality traits identified by psychologist Raymond B. Cattell and others. These traits include warmth, reasoning, emotional stability, social boldness, sensitivity, vigilance, openness to change, self-reliance, perfectionism, dominance, liveliness, rule consciousness, abstractedness, privacy, perfectionism, and tension.[4]

The DISC Assessment

The DISC Personality Test inventory is based on four primary behavioral styles (Dominance, Influence, Steadiness, Conscientiousness), each with a distinct and predictable pattern of observable behavior. The understanding of DISC patterns are used in the hiring process and by those who are in leadership, management, sales, or employee development. All DISC assessments have been researched, developed, and validated by Inscape Publishing, with the Everything DISC assessment model most recently updated in June 2012.[5]

Caliper Profile Index

The Caliper Profile Index (CPI) measures an individual's characteristics, potential, and motivation. This personality test measures 23 personality attributes that are analyzed in a variety of combinations to determine how someone will perform in a specific role.

The CPI is scored over 18 scales which look at different aspects of the applicant's lifestyle and personality. These scales are grouped into the following classes: poise, ascendancy, self-assurance and interpersonal adequacy, socialization, responsibility, intrapersonal values and character, achievement potential, intellectual efficiency, intellectual modes, and interest modes.[6]

Other Personality Tests

Companies sometimes use the following tests during the hiring process because they can help determine what type of personality you have and which industries are the best match for your strengths. These tests can help you and the companies that hire you understand how you are "hardwired." The results offer potential matches to industries or positions that you may never have considered before and in which you could potentially thrive.

The Myers-Briggs Type Indicator® (MBTI®)

This assessment is a questionnaire based on the theories of the Swiss psychiatrist, Carl Jung. It was developed by a mother/daughter team, Katherine Cook Briggs and Isabel Briggs Myers, who used Jung's theory "to enable individuals to grow through an understanding and appreciation of individual differences in healthy personality and to enhance harmony and productivity among diverse groups." For more information, go to www.myers briggs.org

The MBTI indicates how people perceive the world and make decisions. Many Fortune 500 companies have used the MBTI® instrument as part of their management development programs. The MBTI sorts personality preferences in the following ways:

- Extraversion (E) and Introversion (I): Differentiates people who direct their energy primarily outward toward other people and events *from* people who direct their energy inward toward inner environment, thoughts, and experiences.

- Sensing (S) and Intuition (N): Differentiates people who take in information primarily through the five senses and immediate experience *from* people who take in information primarily through hunches and impressions and are more interested in future possibilities.
- Thinking (T) and Feeling (F): Differentiates people who make decisions primarily based on logic and objectivity *from* people who make decisions based on personal values and the effects their decisions will have on others.
- Judging (J) and Perceiving (P): Differentiates people who prefer structure, plans, and achieving closure quickly *from* people who prefer flexibility, spontaneity, and keeping their options open.[7]

I would also recommend *Do What You Are: Discover the Perfect Career for You Through the Secrets of Personality Type, Revised and Updated Edition Featuring E-Careers for the 21st Century,* written by Paul D. Tieger and Barbara Barron-Tieger.

The Strong Interest Inventory®

The Strong assessment measures career and leisure interests. It is based on the work of E. K. Strong, Jr., who first published his inventory on the measurement of interests in 1927. The assessment is often used to aid people in making educational and career decisions. The Strong assessment measures interests in four main categories of scales: General Occupational Themes (GOTs), Basic Interest Scales (BISs), Personal Style Scales (PSSs), and Occupational Scales (OSs).[8]

The Fundamental Interpersonal Relations Orientation–Behavior™ (FIRO-B)

This test was created in the late 1950s by William Schutz, PhD. He developed the FIRO-B theory to aid in the understanding and predicting of how high-performance military teams would work together. The FIRO-B instrument measures behaviors driven by interactive needs in three areas— Inclusion, Control, and Affection—and addresses how such behaviors can affect one's interactions with others. The FIRO-B model is based on the theory that fulfillment of these interpersonal needs serves as motivation in people's daily functioning.[9]

Can You Outsmart a Personality Test?

There is no effective way to cheat on a personality test. Remember, the reliability of these tests have been proven time and time again, and there is sophisticated information embedded in the questions. The best thing to do is be yourself. Follow your instinct. Respond to the question with the first answer that comes to mind. It is important to be honest when taking these tests so you don't end up in a job that you hate. Inconsistent answers to similar questions that are posed several times during each test may also disqualify you from advancing in the hiring process.

Don't try to overanalyze the questions or try to anticipate the *correct answer*. Providing *real answers* to the hypothetical situations posed on these tests is a true indication of how you would respond to the real situation on the job. Once you realize that you cannot beat the test, you can relax and answer the questions as they are posed. If you try to discern the best answer, you will almost always be wrong. Your personality results will ring hollow and the inconsistencies will stick out like a sore thumb.

Although you really can't study effectively for a personality test, you can practice by using sample tests available online. There is very little downside to taking sample tests. You may be able to find similar free versions of the test by searching online the term "free + the name of the report.[10]

Currently, employers have thousands of candidates for positions they post. There is little, if any, bargaining power when it comes to taking a personality test.

My advice? Be yourself, relax, take the test, and if you do not get the position, it probably was not right for you in the first place. Stand tall, be proud, and move on to the next opportunity.

To give yourself a quick test to get an overview of where your personal values rank when looking for the right fit in a working environment, complete the inventory in Exhibit 8-1.

Exhibit 8-1　Personal Values Inventory

Personal values have an impact on your decision making and satisfaction regarding relationships and making the "right fit." To gain better insight into the values that shape your personal choices or that may disconnect your contribution in a particular working environment, rank each value in terms of its importance to you.

VALUE	DEFINITION	HIGH	MEDIUM	LOW
		IMPORTANCE TO YOU		
Accomplishment	Making things happen; getting results, mastery			
Challenge	Taking risks; willingness to test the unknown			
Collaboration	Working together; building on ideas with others			
Ingenuity	Seeing unlimited options; novel ideas; intuition			
Craftsmanship	Being deep in the process, precision, and completion of the final product			
Dependability	Being a reliable source of stability and comfort			
Education	Quest for knowledge			
Celebrity	Limelight, fame, reputation			
Harmony	Working and living without conflict			
Health	Physical well-being			
Honesty	Sincerity, openness, authenticity			
Idealism	Striving for things to be better; aiming for perfection			
Identity	Sense of self deriving from culture, traditions, rituals, symbols			
Independence	Autonomy; doing it your way; freedom			
Inner Balance	Among body, mind, spirit, and emotions			
Integrity/Ethics	Sense of believing in and doing "the right thing"			
Life Balance	Self, family, community, society, career			
Love	Deep intimate attachment to another			
Personal Growth	Self-awareness; growing beyond boundaries			
Enjoyment	Fun, pleasure, feeling good			
Control	Ability to make choices, influence others; exercise power and authority for			
Pragmatism	Realism; world view based on facts			
Promotion	Advancement; external evidence of progress			
Recognition	Acknowledgment by others			
Responsibility	Accountability and ownership			

Security	Geographical; financial; emotional			
Spirituality	Belief in a higher being			
Spontaneity	Ability to live fully in the moment; free spirit			
Tenacity	Persistence in the face of obstacles			
Fortune	Accumulation of money; being wealthy			

CHECKLIST

Chapter 8—Personality Testing

_____ Do you understand personality testing?

_____ Have you tested yourself with the various online samples of different personality tests?

_____ Are you comfortable responding with the first thing that comes to mind when you are taking a personality test, instead of trying to cheat?

_____ Have you gone a step further and read Do What You Are? (written by Paul D, Tieger and Barbara Barron-Tieger)

_____ Have you began to consider industries or positions you may have never thought of before as a result?

_____ Do you have a better idea of the way you communicate to others and the way you like people to communicate with you?

_____ Has personality testing revealed how you are "hardwired" and what your natural strengths and weaknesses are?

_____ Have you considered having a certified test administrator help you interpret the results of any of the personality tests?

9

Personal Marketing Plan

Your personal marketing plan is a two-page strategy that summarizes your job search. The Personal Marketing Plan (PMP) you create will provide an overview of your strategy that details how you are going to position yourself in the job market (see Exhibit 9-1). It is a flexible document to be adjusted over time to reflect what you have learned during your job search. Your PMP will serve as a road map to reemployment. I recommend you read it twice each job search day: once at the start and again at the end. Your PMP provides focus and will help eliminate distractions; it will reinforce the key aspects and goals of your job search.

To be competitive in the marketplace, recognize that in the eyes of employers you are both a person *and* a product with unique talents and abilities. Even the finest products won't succeed without a strong marketing strategy. Your personal marketing plan begins with an overall, yet flexible, design; an understanding of your target audience in the marketplace; and a focus on the types of employers who are looking for someone with your qualifications. Ask yourself, "Are my target companies all within one industry or are there multiple industries that would hire employees with my skills and background?"

The Essential Parts of Your Marketing Plan

The key elements in creating an effective personal marketing plan are your:

- Bridge statement
- Career summary

- 30-second commercial
- Personalized stationery
- Business cards
- Your unique Differential Advantages
- Sources and resources to locate potential employers
- List of target companies
- LinkedIn profile (see Chapter 17, "Social Networking")

Exhibit 9-1 Personal Marketing Plan

NAME: _____

ADDRESS: _____

CITY, STATE ZIP CODE: _____

****

BRIDGE STATEMENT: _____

TITLE: _____

WITH EXTENSIVE EXPERIENCE IN: _____

_____

CAREER SUMMARY:

_____

30-SECOND COMMERCIAL:

_____

_____

PERSONALIZED STATIONERY

BUSINESS CARDS

MY UNIQUE DIFFERENTIAL ADVANTAGE:

_____

_____

Bridge Statement

A bridge statement is *a nonemotional* account of what happened when you lost your job. This statement creates a "bridge" connecting your job loss to your current status and then indicates the direction in which you are heading. Think of it as the answer to the question, "What really happened?"

You build a bridge statement around the facts. No matter why you were let go (personality conflict, new management, downsizing), it is perfectly okay to use phrases like "there was a reorganization, and I was affected." Here are some examples of effective bridge statements:

- "My new boss and I were like oil and water. This never happened to me before, and I hope it never happens again." It is very common to have a personality conflict at least once in a career.

- "As you may have a read in the paper, my former company announced downsizing of over 2,500 employees. I was one of those affected by the company's reorganization." Note that this statement speaks in a believable, nonemotional way. By sharing the fact that over 2,500 employees were affected by the downsizing, you reinforce the idea that you were a part of an overall reorganization, that you did nothing wrong, and that your job loss was not related in any way to your performance or ability to get things done.

- "You may not be aware that the ABC Plant is closing. Senior management decided to move all operations to Mexico. Only ten people are moving; the rest of us are looking for jobs. It was a great position, the company was terrific, and we were all sad to see it move." A bridge statement like this demonstrates the realities of the economy. Sadly, plant closings (because of mergers, consolidations, and outsourcing) demonstrate that manufacturing is quickly becoming obsolete in America—a trend you have no control over. Your bridge statement, however, presents the facts: you were part of a production plant closing.

Career Summary

Your career summary is a strategic series of sentences that provide an overall view of who you are professionally. It is *forward-looking* and summarizes who you are, what you have accomplished, and where you are targeting yourself to go next. Your summary should be packed with key words to ensure your résumé gets read by another person. Think of it as a positioning statement— your career summary sets the platform for your job search campaign.

When I am working with a member at Professionals in Transition® Support Group Inc. (PIT®), I recommended developing a career summary using the following format:

- *TITLE* (insert a career title: Analyst, Sales Manager, Operations Professional, Chemical Engineer—whatever your position or career direction might be)
- *With EXTENSIVE EXPERIENCE in:* _____, _____, _____, *and* _____.
  Sample: Extensive experiences in specific strategic marketing plans across multiple types of businesses including service, retail, financial, real estate, restaurant, and not-for-profit. Or, experienced in direct mail, web-based email advertising, proofing, color correcting, retouching, printing, and development of corporate promotional materials.
- *FUNCTIONAL SKILLS*—These are the things you did every day.
  Sample: Functional skills include customer database marketing, social media, newspaper, and trade advertising. *Note:* This is optional and may not always be necessary.
  OTHER SKILLS in _____, _____, and _____.
  Sample: Additional skills in problem solving and cost control; dedicated and dependable professional who motivates others and produces quality work on time or ahead of schedule.
- *CLOSING SUMMARY*
  Sample: Methodical and adaptive worker with strong communication and organization skills, able to achieve project success in teams or as individual assignments.

30-Second Commercial

As a subset of your career summary, your 30-second commercial *condenses* your career down to the most important of the important. You can determine how much needs to be abridged by reading your career summary out loud and timing yourself. Slow down as you read it, because those who will hear your 30-second commercial need a few seconds to process the information. (See Exhibits 9-2A and 9-2B) You don't want to overwhelm your audience with too much information. Instead you want them to remember you. Make it easy by giving them a business card with your career summary restated and your contact information.

Personalized Stationery

Personal stationery uses your contact information to create formal letterhead that is personalized. Simply highlight the personal information at the top of your résumé and then paste it in the center of a blank page. To create visual attention, make your name larger than your mailing address, telephone number, email addresses, and LinkedIn profile address. Set your name in 14 to 16 point Times Roman or Arial boldface type.

Exhibit 9-2A   Your 30-Second Commercial

- Your name
- What you've been doing (transferrable skills)
- What you're looking to do
- What kind of assistance/information you are looking for (if needed)

Your name	My name is Marion Smith
What you've been doing	I have been working in sales management for several years with my most recent position being VP of Sales and Marketing for ATC Enterprises. At ATC, I marketed information technology services to the energy industry.
What you're looking to do	I'm exploring new opportunities in business development in the IT industry, with a focus on web based organizations.
What kind of assistance/information you are looking for	
The way you could help me is . . . (customize to the contact)	

Exhibit 9-2B   Information Beyond the 30-Second Commercial

When You Need to Give More Information

Your networking conversations may develop into a longer conversation and your 30-second commercial will become your two-minute commercial. This will occur in almost any interview-like situation where you are asked to. . .

"Tell Me a Little More About Yourself"

Time: ± 60 Seconds - WORK HISTORY
- In chronological or reverse chronological order, summarize your work experience, giving company names and titles if appropriate.
- Emphasize key areas of responsibility and major accomplishments. Devote the most time to your most recent position.
- SAY WHAT YOU DO BEST AND GIVE EXAMPLES

Time: ±15 Seconds - Additional Inquiry:
- WHAT HAPPENED? ▶ YOUR PUBLIC STATEMENT
- WHAT NOW? ▶ BRIDGE TO TODAY

Time: ± 15 Seconds - PERSONAL BACKGROUND (Only If Asked)
- Where you were born and where did you grow up
- Your education, military experience if applicable, and additional training or continuing education
- **REMEMBER: A potential employer is interested in what you can do for the company, not in your personal history.**

With this letterhead, your written communications are professional and consistent with your résumé. Save your letterhead as a template, so that you can use it to create documents as you need them.

The easiest and most cost-effective way to create a business card is by designing and buying them online. I have had great success making my own business cards at www.Vistaprint.com. Other sites to consider include www.zazzle.com, www.staples.com, www.businesscards24.com, and www.businesscardland.com. You can find additional sites by performing a general search for business cards in your search engine. Each site offers easy to use business card templates. For examples of business cards, see Exhibit 9-3.

Exhibit 9-3   Sample Business Card

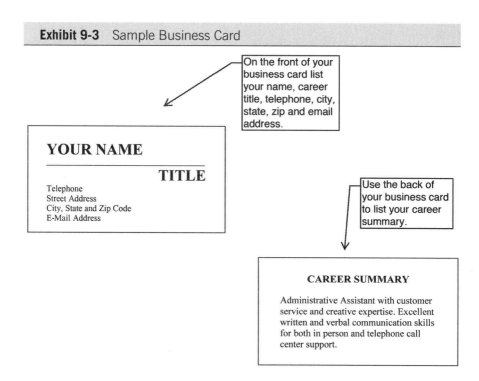

Be cautious of "free" business cards. Be sure to read the fine print carefully. In many cases there is a hefty postage and handling fee, as well as other fees for customization. However, it still costs less (in most cases) than having the cards professionally printed.

You can also make your own business cards using Microsoft Word or Publisher and then print them yourself. All of the office supply stores sell templates and business card stock provided by Avery. Learn more at: http://www.avery.com/avery/en_US/Projects-&-Ideas/Ideas-for-Work/Business-Communications/Articles/Do_It_Yourself-Business-Cards.htm

Your Unique Differential Advantage

Your unique differential advantage can be defined as those strategic benefits and experience that *only you can provide*. Understanding and marketing those distinctive qualities is the key to standing above the crowd. It strengthens and better positions you in a competitive business environment.

Market your strengths by using your exclusive abilities. These skills allow you to create a unique platform based on your individual expertise. Focusing your job search around your unique differential advantage enables you to eliminate 95 percent of the positions you do not qualify for, thus allowing you to concentrate on the 5 percent of jobs that do require your skills and talents.

Concentrating on your unique skills will create momentum as you move forward in your job search. It will reduce frustration, save time and energy, and help to quickly eliminate dead ends. By investing the time to figure out your differential advantage, you will save hours of time and reduce the overall length of time you are out of work.

List of Target Companies

It is important to create a list of companies you want to target for job opportunities (see Exhibit 9-4). Once you have determined which companies meet your search criteria, your goal is to get inside those companies through your existing network or future networking contacts. Your aim is to meet the hiring managers, not HR personnel. There will be plenty of time to meet HR later.

This is opposite to what most job seekers do. To create a target company list, you must invest time and "pinpoint" what types of organizations you most want to join. Start with a wide selection of industry categories with which your skills, experiences, and interests would be a good fit. Examples might include manufacturing, sales, operations, or consumer products. Gather as much material on your targeted companies as you can and start the networking process. Your list should contain 35 to 50 company names segmented into distinct categories or industries. The sooner you aim at specific employers, the sooner you'll get to meet decision makers at these firms.

As you make contact within your network of potential information sources, "jog the memory" of each person so he or she will give you the names of and contact information for people they know in your targeted companies. This means you'll have "warm referrals" in your targeted companies rather than having to rely on "cold calls."

Exhibit 9-4   Target Companies Information Sheet

TARGET COMPANIES - INFORMATION SHEET SAMPLE

Systematically record the information you gather about your target companies through networking, reading, and researching. Keep all important information and dates in one convenient
location. You might want to make a target-company information and contact sheet for each
company or you might prefer index cards.

Company name _____

Address _____

Website _____

Telephone Blog _____

Sales volume _____

Number of employees _____

Location(s) _____

Products/services _____

Contact's name _____ Contact's assistant _____

Comments _____

_____

_____

Date _____ Call-back date _____

You can use the following techniques to begin researching your target
companies:

- Talk to friends, family, colleagues, and neighbors who might know
  the "inside scoop" at some of your target companies.
- Network to find current or past employees at your target companies.
- Hear personally what the organization is like from the inside out.
- Review *Fortune* Magazine's list of 100 Great Places to Work in Amer-
  ica (www.greatplacetowork.com).
- Read local editions of the *Business Journal* (www.bizjournals.com).

- Consult business articles in your local daily newspaper's business section.
- Access social networking websites that connect you with other professionals and offer company information (e.g., www.linkedin.com).
- Contact your local Chambers of Commerce, trade associations, and industry organizations to which your target company might belong.
- Check websites of and downloadable annual reports from your target companies.
- Use Google to do a search on the company and its executives and see what kinds of articles and stories come-up (www.google.com).
- Go to your local library which may give you free access to databases that are usually fee-based, such as Hoover's Master List of Major U.S. Corporations, Dun & Bradstreet's Million Dollar Directory, www .Vault.com, www.ReferenceUSA.com, and www.OneSource.com.
- In addition, there is a great article by Ford R. Myers that provides additional suggestions on how to further build your target list.[1]

The mere fact you have invested the time to create a target company list demonstrates you are professional and organized. You've "done your homework." It also distinguishes you from other job-seekers because you have developed your personal marketing plan (PMP).

CHECKLIST

Chapter 9—Personal Marketing Plan

_____ Do you recognize that you are a marketable product?
_____ Have you prepared your bridge statement?
_____ What are your unique, differential advantages?
_____ What marketing tools do you need?
_____ Have you developed a target list of companies?
_____ Did you refine your "30-second commercial"?
_____ Have you developed a career summary?

Crafting an Effective Résumé

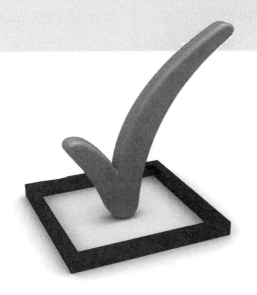

CHECKLIST 1

Understand the types of résumé formats.
____   Chronological.
____   Functional.
____   Review samples of strong résumés.
____   Develop an impressive mission statement.
____   Seek electronic keywords (program search).
          Create a concise career summary.
          ____   Develop three to four key accomplishments per work
               experience.
____   Emphasize your skills (transferrable skills).
____   *Do not* provide personal information.
____   *Do not* list references.
____   *Proofread . . . proofread . . .* and *proofread* again.
          Correct and eliminate typos, errors, and misspellings.
____   Ask for an outside reviewer to check your résumé. . . . Make it short,
          simple, and complete.
____   Take responsibility for yourself. . . . Know thyself.

CHECKLIST 2

Understand the basic structure of a cover letter.
          ____   T-square letter . . . "requirements" to "skills."
____   Review strong, dynamic cover letters.
____   Customize cover letters to specific needs.
____   Address to a named individual not a job title.
____   Request action.
____   *Proofread . . . proofread . . .* and *proofread* again.
          Correct and eliminate typos, errors, and misspellings.
          Complete online applications.
          ____   Utilize .txt format to combine your cover letter and résumé
               for continuous flow of information.
____   Follow up once your application has been submitted. . . . Be
          persistent.
____   Understand the Emotional Wave of Unemployment.
          (99 No's for each Yes . . . Depression . . . Hitting bottom)

10

Résumé Components

There's no such thing as a perfect résumé. After writing thousands of résumés for job seekers, I can tell you there is *no golden ticket* or *magic résumé*, but there are universal features that will help you rise above the masses. Once you understand the key components, or universal segments, of a résumé, you will be able to determine whether you want to write a chronological or a functional résumé (see Chapter 11, "Chronological or Functional Résumés"). A well-written résumé is critical to your success and serves as your platform for marketing your personal brand, which is <u>You</u>. It is your primary job-search communication tool and is well worth the time it takes to make it effective. Your résumé has multiple purposes:

- It gives a candid snapshot of your background and highlights your skills and accomplishments by means of a self-assessment checklist (see Exhibit 10-1).
- It serves as a marketing platform for the brand *You*.
- It empowers you to work around HR by networking directly with key decision makers.
- It can act as an agenda for an interviewer to use as a guide to your background and serves as a launch point for additional conversation and/or questions.
- It demonstrates major work-related issues you have proactively managed and resolved.
- It presents to an employer your "on-the-job" experiences relative to the position for which you are interviewing.

Exhibit 10-1 Self-Assessment Checklist

For help in remembering your achievements, answer the questions listed below. When answering, think of all aspects of your life, not just work (for example, volunteer and church activities).

1. What awards or commendations have you received and what accomplishments did they celebrate?

2. Have you been recognized for a good work record or perfect attendance?

3. What achievements led to your being promoted from one job to another?

4. What on-the-job training programs have you completed?

5. What work-related training courses have you attended?

6. Which of your contributions to your company resulted in personal recognition? Why were your contributions advantageous to the company?

7. Have you been involved in a team effort that produced a specific result?

8. How have you influenced the direction, efficiency, or productivity of a work group?

9. Describe a change initiative that you implemented.

10. Describe a coalition or project team that you built.

11. List ways you have saved your employer time or money.

12. What have you done to help others reach their goals?

13. How have you increased sales? How have you reduced costs?

14. What action did you take or what contribution did you make regarding a company decision or change?

15. Describe how you discovered and met a need.

16. Tell about a time when you achieved a goal by following instructions.

17. Explain how you showed leadership during a challenging situation.

18. Describe an instance in which you developed an idea.

19. Give an example of something you created or built.

20. Describe a situation in which you solved a problem or took charge of an emergency.

- It documents major actions or decisions you have made throughout your career and measures the results of your involvement both methodically and quantitatively.
- It pinpoints events and highlights achievements in your career.
- It creates opportunities to demonstrate transferrable skills and personal achievements relative to the job for which you are applying.

Aren't all résumés basically the same? No, they are not. An individual's accomplishments are like their fingerprints—no two are alike. The truth is that top-notch résumé formats from career counseling organizations across the United States are similar in style. Any minor differences in formatting are only cosmetic. A résumé's uniqueness is achieved by presenting your transferrable skills and experiences.

The bottom line is that all effective résumés share key universal segments.

Universal Résumé Segments

Regardless of the type of résumé you write, combining these universal segments effectively will create a clear, clean, and concise document that will be easy to scan, simple to understand, and visually friendly (see Exhibit 10-2).

Universal résumé segments guide a reader's eyes through the résumé by creating logical sections. The margins are wide, the style of lettering easy to read, and the type sizes are generous. After more than twenty years, I have found that regardless of the type of résumé you choose, all résumés should have the five universal segments listed below; they should be bold and capitalized (see Exhibit 10-2):

- Name
- Career Summary
- Areas of Expertise
- Professional Experience
- Education

Exhibit 10-2   Universal Résumé Segments

NAME
9999 Anywhere Drive
City, State, Zip Code
Your name@yahoo.com

SUMMARY

Bottom-line oriented Marketing and Sales Professional with extensive experience in both domestic and international chemical markets. Special skills in building motivated sales organizations; repositioning products for increased profitability; analyzing; and negotiating acquisitions. Highly developed communication and design skills; Known as the "go-to" person for innovative ideas and solutions; and Resourceful, persistent, creative.

AREAS OF EXPERTISE

• Key Word	• Key Word	• Key Word
• Key Word	• Key Word	• Key Word
• Key Word	• Key Word	• Key Word

HIGHLIGHT OF ACHIEVEMENTS

- Grew $4 million adhesives manufacturing business to $56 million, with 16% earnings and 23% return on capital.
- Positioned specialty chemical group retail product line from a zero base to the second leading brand in its category.

RÉSUMÉ GUIDELINES

Keep It Short

Fifteen years or more of solid work experience *entitles you to a two-page résumé*. Remember, however, you do not have to itemize all your qualifications. If you leave the employer interested in gathering more information, he or she may call to get it, and that's exactly what you want—a phone call giving you the opportunity to establish rapport and, ultimately, earn a job interview.

Keep It Simple

Industry jargon or acronyms may confuse the person in HR who screens your résumé. If the reader does not understand your résumé, there is a high likelihood it will be passed over. Note that a majority of résumés are now reviewed by software programs that search for specific, position-related keywords. If your résumé does not contain any of these keywords, it will not be flagged for review (see Chapter 12, "Keywords: The Hidden Language of the Internet")

A Technology Résumé Is Different

Many hiring managers tell me that on a technology résumé they want to see both hardware and software skills listed below the career summary to ensure that the applicant has the minimum qualifications required before they read further. Therefore, those of you in a technical environment should list technical terms/references (e.g., C++, mainframe, CICS) in an Area of Expertise section on your résumé.

Front-Load Important Information

From an employer's point of view, the ability to skim your résumé is vital. *Your Career Summary * Areas of Expertise * Job Experience * Education* will probably be all he or she has time to scan in fifteen to thirty seconds. Assume they will concentrate on your last 10 years and skim the rest. *Your challenge is to slow the reader down* by putting your most important and interesting information first. Potential employers are looking for measurable benefits you have accomplished throughout your career. Your résumé will rise to the top of the pile if both HR and hiring managers find it easy to see your relevance and the value you have contributed to companies in the past.

Quantify Your Most Important Achievements

Adding specifics as "increased sales by 20%" or "cut response time in half" helps bring your most important work experiences into focus and adds to your credibility. Always write in a third tense and describe your accomplishments using *action words* such as:

Achieved	Composed	Facilitated	Maintained	Sold
Allocated	Conducted	Formulated	Mediated	Staffed
Anticipated	Consolidated	Generated	Negotiated	Streamlined
Assigned	Counseled	Handled	Organized	Summarized
Awarded	Delegated	Identified	Purchased	Traced
Assisted	Defined	Headed	Planned	Taught
Balanced	Designed	Improved	Revised	Tracked
Built	Developed	Invented	Secured	Used
Chaired	Established	Launched	Selected	Verified
Compiled	Evaluated	Lead	Served	Wrote

Leave Your Personal Life Out

The older you are, the less important your hobbies, group affiliations, and even education become. Focus instead on skills and experiences that best sell *you* to an employer. Never include your age, marital status, or social security number. Do not provide references until asked for in a second or third interview. You want to control information going to your references. It is important to "feed and nourish" your references by providing regular updates on your progress. When a company asks for references, be sure to give each of them a "heads up" call. Orient them about the position and company you interviewed with and ask your referrals if they would like a suggested script to follow when they are contacted.

Eliminate Nonessential Words

Your writing style should be direct and to the point. Edit and eliminate any nonessential information. Less is really more. The person skimming your résumé will be grateful for your brevity and ability to get to the point. So, present your qualifications in as few words as possible. Remember that an HR professional will spend sixty seconds or less scanning your résumé. Keep it crisp, clean, concise, and visually friendly.

Include Only What Feels Comfortable

You should be able to elaborate on your résumé when you're invited for an interview. Your résumé is a forward-looking document and should not include information about unpleasant or tedious job responsibilities. Highlight those achievements you are proud of. Quantifiable, measurable benefits make your résumé interesting. Readers will slow down naturally and pause on achievements of interest to them. A benefit-driven résumé will showcase your unique talents and abilities, and this will really make it "pop."

Make It User Friendly

Guide readers through your résumé by using bullet points. Make it easy on the eyes by using generous margins and a type size large enough to read without a magnifying glass. I recommend Times New Roman or Arial, with a font size of 11 or 12 (no smaller). Don't clutter your résumé with multiple fonts or an abundance of italics, boldfacing, or underlining. Instead, create a vibrant and tasteful presentation that clearly communicates your qualifications and abilities and reflects your work experience.

Remember the "One-Screen Rule"

HR managers have told me of a "one-screen rule." If they open your résumé, they usually review only that portion that fits on one computer screen. This means that the only information they see is your contact information and career summary; and perhaps an expertise section. If they do not immediately see what they are looking for, chances are they will stop reading. (See Exhibit 10-2 Universal Résumé Segments for an example of focusing your readers to the top 1/3 portion of your résumé.)

T-Square Cover Letters

I have been told by students and clients that their response rate increased by 60 percent when a strong universal résumé was accompanied by a complimentary "T-square" cover letter (see Exhibit 10-3). It is called a T-square cover letter because the letter "T" is formed by the horizontal line that underscores "your requirements" and "my experience" and the vertical line that divides the two columns.

A cover letter is a written introduction of YOU; a T-square cover letter presents your experiences as a potential match with the qualifications an

Exhibit 10-3   T-Square Cover Letter

YOUR NAME
Address, City, State Zip Code
Telephone/Cell Number   Email Address

9/99/9999

Mr. Phillip Smith
VP, Engineering
ABC Corporation
One Industry Plaza
Anytown, NY 12096

Dear Mr. Smith:

I have more than seven years of engineering experience and am responding to your recent advertisement for a Project Engineer. While my résumé is enclosed, I have highlighted below how my skills relate to your stated requirements.

YOUR REQUIREMENTS	MY EXPERIENCE
A recognized engineering degree plus several years of practical experience	Obtained a BS degree in Mechanical Engineering from NC State University and have more than seven years of practical experience.
Excellent people skills and demonstrated ability to motivate staff.	Excellent people skills and demonstrated abilities to motivate a staff of five.
Strong administrative and analytical skills.	Proven administrative and analytical skills.
Good oral and written communication skills.	Trained two new technicians via daily coaching sessions, communication meetings and technical skill sessions.

I believe my background provides the skills you require for this position. I would welcome the chance for a personal interview with you to further discuss my qualifications and will call you next week to determine the best time for us to meet.

Sincerely,

YOUR NAME
Enclosure

employer is looking for to fill an open position. The cover letter provides a snapshot of your résumé—your personal information (on your personalized letterhead), directed to a particular individual at a specific company, providing the title of the available position and how you learned about it (online, print advertisement, or personal recommendation).

The focus of the T-square cover letter is to match your experience to the job requirements. This quick snapshot allows the HR representative or outside recruiter to quickly match the positions "must haves" with your qualifications. Even if Automatic Tracking System software is employed to electronically scan for keywords, this match of experience to requirements is an easy way to identify potential applicants.

The T-square cover letter provides your introduction to the attached detailed résumé of your skills and experiences. What better way of making a first impression of qualification and thereby entice the recipient to read deeper into your résumé.

CHECKLIST 1

Chapter 10—Résumé Components

_____ Do you have an up-to-date, concise, and easy-to-read résumé? (More than just a chronological listing of your experience.)

_____ Have you included all the universal résumé segments?

_____ Do your experiences and achievements support your career summary?

_____ Have you quantified your achievements or results?

_____ Does your résumé meet the one-screen rule?

_____ Have you checked and rechecked spelling, grammar, and punctuation?

CHECKLIST 2

Chapter 10—Effective Cover Letters

Understand the basic structure of a cover letter.

_____   T-square letter matching "requirements" to "experience."

_____   Use action verbs to describe accomplishments.

_____   Address cover letter to a named individual.

_____   Customize cover letter to specific needs of each employer.

_____   Clearly define how you can meet the employer's needs.

_____   Focus cover letter with specific information.

_____   Request action from the employer.

_____   *Proofread . . . proofread . . .* and *proofread* again.

Correct and eliminate typos, errors, and misspellings.

11

Chronological or Functional Résumé?

Your résumé is an organized written presentation of you—of your relevant information and accomplishments specifically targeted toward your job search. *It is not a laundry list of jobs.* Instead, it is a clear, concise professional picture of you and your work history.

- Determine your format below and stick with it.
- Use bulleted statements and avoid long paragraphs. Don't bore your reader.
  - Avoid using "responsible for," "duties include," or "responsibilities include."
  - Avoid using personal pronouns—I, me, my.
  Remember: It is the reader's perception of you that will make an impact.
- Use a large enough font that is easy to read.

Chronological Résumé

A chronological résumé lists all your positions starting with the most recent and working backward in reverse chronological order (see Exhibit 11-1). Chronological résumés are used 95 percent of the time.

(text continues on page 120)

Exhibit 11-1   Chronological Résumé

NAME
9999 Anywhere Drive
City, State, Zip Code
your name@yahoo.com

SUMMARY

Your career summary serves as your 30-second commercial and, in five sentences or less, sets the overall tone of your résumé. It positions you in the marketplace and pulls from the body of your résumé industry specific terms, key words, and core transferrable skills. The summary translates your skills into a brief series of powerful sentences and organizes the information the reader is about to read. All other résumé information defends your career summary by providing details of your specific career achievements.

AREAS OF EXPERTISE

• Key Word	• Key Word	• Key Word
• Key Word	• Key Word	• Key Word
• Key Word	• Key Word	• Key Word

PROFESSIONAL EXPERIENCE

LAST EMPLOYER, Location   **Years from-to**
Last Formal Title

A brief summary of your stated responsibilities. This should be phrased much like your formal "job description." Remember that your next employer is usually more interested in what you did rather than for whom you did it. Save the "how well" you did it for the bulleted list below.

- Highlight the accomplishments of your position by using bullets. Bulleted items *must* contain key words and numbers.
- Use direct, easy-to-read sentences, such as: "Created *X*, resulting in *Y*.
- Keep in mind that you are creating these statements of accomplishment to support the claims you've made above in your summary.
- Remember, a team accomplishment is also YOUR accomplishment.
- Accomplishments are not solely related to sales and revenues. Did you create or improve a process or procedure, a person or department, a relationship? Did you reduce a cost/expense? Did you improve information flow or efficiency?
- Think about everything you were rated on for your annual review.

SECOND LAST GREAT EMPLOYER, Location   **Years from-to**
Formal Title

The best place to pull information for a general description of your position is from your performance appraisal. You want to demonstrate your effectiveness by providing quantifiable, measurable benefits. Each bulleted point gives you an opportunity to tell a story about your performance and quickly establish rapport with interviewer.

- Employers concentrate their time on the last ten years of your experience. When allocating bulleted points, plan six for your most recent employer and 4 to 5 for your second last employer.
- More really is less. Make sure that you follow this format to create an eye-friendly document that features generous margins and good flow.
- Your résumé needs to convince someone who does not know you that you have the right stuff.
- A problem requiring action that brought tangible results should be summarized in bullet points. Problem-action-reult statements highlight skill sets that demonstrate how you made a difference in the companies you have worked for.

THIRD LAST GREAT EMPLOYER, Location   **Years from-to**
Formal Title

Supporting jobs don't require as much space. Your résumé should reflect the building of your career. However, the bulleted points that you document should be as impressive as possible given the level of your responsibility at the time.

- The farther you go into your résumé, the fewer bulleted points you will need.
- However, each bulleted point (regardless of where it is located creates opportunities to demonstrate transferable skills and personal achievements as it applies to the job you are interviewing for.
- Your goal is to show consistent performance throughout your career.

FOURTH LAST GREAT EMPLOYER, Location   **Years from-to**
Formal Title

When you have the main supporting positions well structured, start minimizing the content of the information.

- At this point you should have 2 to 3 bulleted points
- How long should a résumé be? It should be appropriate to your career.
- Never hide your age.

FIFTH GREAT EMPLOYER, Location   **Years from-to**
Formal Title

A general description of your highest obtained position, with bulleted points listing the other positions held with the same company is fine.

- It is appropriate to list other positions within the same company in bulleted point format with the years that you worked in each position.
- Don't use your résumé for your first job as a guide for your twenty-year career résumé.

EDUCATION

Center the Degree and University, Date optional
BS, Résumé Writing University, 1986

Functional Résumé

A functional résumé emphasizes transferrable skills and achievements while minimizing when and where you have worked (see Exhibit 11-2). Functional résumés are only used 5 percent of the time. Job seekers who might consider using a functional résumé include:

- College students with minimal experience and/or experience unrelated to their chosen career field.
- Individuals whose predominant or most relevant experience has been unpaid, such as volunteer workers or participants in college activities (coursework, class projects, extracurricular organizations, and sports).
- Workers with highly diverse experiences that don't add up to a clearcut career path.
- Career changers who wish to enter a field very different from their previous work experience. In this instance, a chronological résumé would confuse an HR professional because it would present an unfiltered view of your career experiences versus highlighting only the quantifiable measurable benefits from your past that are relevant to the "new" career path you are heading toward.
- Workers with gaps in their work history, such as a mom who put her career on hold and made a commitment to raise her family or perhaps someone who took time to care for an aging parent and now wishes to return to the workplace. A chronological format would marginalize strong, proven, and transferrable skills by drawing undue attention to these time gaps, and in many cases, the résumé would get eliminated long before it would ever hit the desk of a decision maker. On the other hand, a functional résumé quickly demonstrates transferrable skills and abilities obtained throughout a career incorporating any potential concerns during the résumé time gap like domestic management and volunteer work.
- Armed forces veterans reentering a different field from the one in which they performed in the military.

Exhibit 11-2   Functional Résumé

NAME
9999 Anywhere Drive
City, State, Zip Code
your name@yahoo.com

SUMMARY

A functional résumé is used if you have large gaps in your career, are required to have a one-page version of your résumé, or are going in a new career direction. With this type of résumé, your primary task is to de-emphasize the amount of time you were at a particular company and highlight your major work achievements across time. You can use the same career summary as you developed for your chronological résumé or (if changing careers) highlight how your transferrable skills apply to the new industry you have chosen.

AREAS OF EXPERTISE

• Key Word	• Key Word	• Key Word
• Key Word	• Key Word	• Key Word
• Key Word	• Key Word	• Key Word

HIGHLIGHT OF ACHIEVEMENTS

- Lead off with your strongest problem, action, result statement. You will have fewer bulleted points in this format, and you want to grab the reader's attention quickly.
- Use powerful, easy-to-read sentences, such as: "Created X, resulting in Y."
- Keep in mind that you are creating these statements of accomplishment to support your summary. This is particularly important if you are changing careers and "hyping" your transferable skills.
- Be sure to have real world examples of how you used your transferable skills throughout your career and how they would apply to the position in which you are interested.
- Accomplishments are not solely related to sales and revenues. Did you create or improve a process or procedure, a person or department, a relationship? Did you reduce a cost/expense?

JOB EXPERIENCE

LAST GREAT EMPLOYER, Location	Years from-to
SECOND LAST GREAT EMPLOYER, Location	Years from-to
THIRD LAST GREAT EMPLOYER, Location	Years from-to
FOURTH LAST GREAT EMPLOYER, Location	Years from-to
FIFTH LAST GREAT EMPLOYER, Location	Years from-to

EDUCATION
BS, Résumé Writing University

- Workers looking for a position for which a chronological listing could make them look "overqualified"
- Mature workers seeking to deemphasize a lengthy job history

You may be wondering why a functional résumé is not as easily accepted by a company. Some employers may be unaccustomed to seeing a functional format and may become confused or even annoyed. It is your job, however, to position yourself with the strongest and most favorable format possible.

In some cases, headhunters (slang for job recruiters) may not respond positively to a functional résumé. Remember that they work for companies looking to fill positions; they do not work for you. That being said, a chronological résumé (work holes and all) might be a better recommended résumé format. Most recruiters look to fill positions by "stealing" an employee from an existing company.

In addition, be aware that employers in conservative fields, such as finance, banking, and law, and international employers are not huge fans of functional formats. Functional résumés may not be acceptable when applying online (see Chapter 12, "Keywords: The Hidden Language of the Internet"). A chronological format focuses the reader's attention on recent job history and experiences, while a functional format directs the reader's attention to functional strengths and qualifications. The comparison charts in Exhibits 11-3 and 11-4 should help you determine which format is best for you.

Exhibit 11-3   How to Decide Which Résumé Format Is Best for You

Chronological	Functional
• Longevity in the same occupation and/or industry	• Change in career path, such as from corporate to not-for-profits, office to lab technician, factory to nursing
• Career path is steady with progressive responsibilities	• Focus on skills and abilities not currently used or recently obtained (different from previous experience)
• Similar job objective(s)	• Different job objective(s)
• Previous employers have been prominent/ prestigious	• Experience(s) gained in different, unrelated jobs or volunteer fields
• Employed by the same company for a very long time	• Employed by a number of companies with some gaps in between.
• Work history has unbroken employment record/no gaps	• Frequent job hopping
	• Entering the job market after an absence

Exhibit 11-4   Comparison of Chronological and Functional Résumé Features

Chronological	Functional
1. Name/Address/Phone/Email	1. Name/Address/Phone/Email
2. Areas of Expertise	2. Areas of Expertise
3. Summary	3. Summary
4. Professional experience, documented as measurable benefits	4. Selected accomplishments listed under specific functional areas of expertise
5. Volunteer activities (optional)	5. Professional experience
6. Military service	6. Volunteer activities (optional)
7. Computer Skills	7. Military service
8. Education and training	8. Computer skills (technical detail)
9. Memberships/associations	9. Education and training
	10. Memberships/Associations

A lead-in paragraph with the first sentence announcing your generic job title and level of responsibility within a functional area of experience and/or industry. The second sentence

(continues)

Exhibit 11-4 *(continued)*
should emphasize and build on technical expertise, critical strengths, contributions, and skills.

Summary: Concise statement summarizing experience, areas of expertise, and technical or professional skills. The summary should use business and/or professional language to indicate level of responsibility, potential contributions to the employer, and greatest strengths.

Accomplishments: Specific examples of success doing a key duty of your job and covering the most important aspect of your job. An accomplishment should answer the question, "How did I work differently or better?" Accomplishments highlight the value, benefits, and contributions you brought to an organization. (Problem . . . Action . . . Result)

Awards: Behind every award is usually an accomplishment. List the award as it increases the impact, power, and effectiveness of your accomplishment.

Volunteer experience: List only if it supports your job search or emphasizes key skills you want to highlight.

Military experience: Important to note, but provide only detail if the experience is relevant to your job search or was for an unusual length of time. Always include branch, dates, rank, and classification.

Education and training: As applicable.

Memberships/associations: Only if relevant to your specific job and space permits.

CHECKLIST

CHAPTER 11—Crafting an Effective Résumé

_____   Do you understand the difference between chronological and functional résumé formats?

Have you:

_____   Developed a powerful career summary (introduction)?
_____   Included key accomplishments for each work experience?
_____   Used bulleted lists and short phrases to describe your accomplishments?
_____   Emphasized your skills (transferrable skills)?
_____   Provided as much contact information as possible?
_____   *Proofread . . . proofread . . .* and *proofread* again.

12

Keywords: The Hidden Language of the Internet

Frequently, decision makers ask me if I know anyone at Professionals in Transition® who would meet the qualifications for a particular position. This is because (in their opinions) they *just can't find good, qualified people.*

This chapter discusses how employers find qualified applicants (long before a person gets involved) by means of electronically screening and tracking résumés—the applicant tracking systems, job aggregators, and keywords, collectively known as the language of the internet.

Applicant Tracking Systems (ATS)

Many employers use an ATS software program to process job applications and manage the entire recruiting process. The database environment is used to:

- Manage the hiring process (start to finish).
- Automatically screen potential applicants.
- Test candidates.
- Schedule interviews.
- Monitor reference checks.
- Complete new-hire paperwork.

An ATS can also be used for regulatory compliance and for tracking sources of candidates—where candidates found the job posting (e.g., from a company website on a job board like Monster.com, directly through a referral from a company employee, or from another source). The majority of job and résumé boards (e.g., Monster, Hotjobs, Career Builder) have partnerships with ATS vendors, who provide the software. The ATS software allows a hiring company to pull your completed application from any of the job boards and transfer it into its system.

How Applicant Tracking Systems Work

With an ATS, applicants upload contact information, experience, and educational background, résumé, and either a cover letter into a job board system or, when applying via a company website, directly to its database. The information is then transferred from one section of the system to another. Once the job seeker's information has been accepted into the company's ATS, the candidate moves through the hiring process.

Depending on a company's hiring practices, an internal or external company recruiter can review the application and decide what next steps (if any) are appropriate. An automated message acknowledging receipt of the application is usually sent. In addition, mandatory online tests (such as the personality tests mentioned or affirmative action statements) can be executed. Another automated step is that the recruiter or a hiring manager can schedule an interview or send a rejection letter with or without actually talking to the applicant. An added benefit of the electronic applicant tracking system for HR personnel is that the same information provided during the application process is automatically uploaded to their personnel and payroll records if an applicant is hired.

ATS software is very efficient and can eliminate hundreds of applications on hundreds of posted job positions with little or no human interaction. Once the parameters (*must haves*) of a position are set, your résumé has little or no chance making it through the initial, automated screening process if you lack the predetermined keywords. ATS programs make hiring a much easier task from an employer's prospective, but are very impersonal for job seekers (sadly taking the "human" out of HR). A great article by Alison Doyle gives more details on ATS.[1]

Keywords: The Language of the Internet

Now that you have an understanding of ATS programs, it is clear that keywords are of critical importance. Keywords, with regard to résumés and job applications, refer to the search terms recruiters and hiring managers use to identify candidates for open positions. Keywords are *a phrase or an abbreviation* for recognized skills. For example, if, MS Office, the abbreviation for Microsoft Office, appears on a résumé, it means the candidate is skilled with products like Word, Excel, PowerPoint, and Outlook.

Keywords can be *industry specific,* like the information technology term "C++," which represents one of the most popular programming languages currently used by companies.[2]

Keywords can define strategic responsibilities like Project Management, Product Implementation, Analysis, Training, or Customer Service.

Keywords also illustrate abilities. Your abilities are compared to the job requirements and then measured against the "keywords" used by a decision maker trying to find the right person to hire. If your résumé does not have any of the correct keywords, it may never be seen by human eyes. ATS filter résumés without judgment or thought. You either have the industry "keywords" or terms or you don't.

Remember that recruiters and hiring managers read *only those résumés or applications that match a job's preset keywords.* With ATS, *there is no independent judgment.* Nobody is at the other end who may read the résumé and think, "Hmmm. . . . This is an interesting résumé. She may not meet have all of the requirements for *this position,* BUT, we could *train her* and then she would qualify for the newly created (but not yet posted) position. She looks good on paper, let's bring her in, and see what she is like in person." Regrettably, those days of recruitment are long gone.

Finding Keywords with a Job Aggregator

An aggregator is a person, association, or object that brings different things or people together. For simplicity's sake, I use only two job aggregators: www.SimplyHired.com and www.Indeed.com.

Johimgren Sundberg, a social media consultant and trainer for recruitment and HR at Link Humans, lists the top job aggregators in order of size.[3] They are:

1. *Indeed.com*

   Started in 2004, Indeed.com was the trailblazer for all job search engines and is still the largest. Indeed.com keeps expanding globally and now offers individualized versions in 19 countries.

2. *SimplyHired.com*

   A close runner up to Indeed and definitely a great contender, SimplyHired looks and feels just like Indeed, but it has more add-on applications that connect you to social media for easy sharing and researching of jobs. It is available in 17 countries worldwide.

3. *CareerJet*

   Again a very similar application to Indeed, CareerJet claims to scan over 58,000 websites daily. Available in more than 50 countries and in 20 languages.

4. *Jobsafari*

   Jobsafari is a European aggregator service available in 10 countries and 8 languages. Covers some countries where other engines are not present.

5. *JobRobot*

   JobRobot is the largest German-language aggregator and is very useful for central European job opportunities.

Pinpointing Keywords That Are Right for You

1. Go to the job aggregator of your choice.
2. Enter your current job title or position.
3. Do not fill in the zip code.
4. Hit enter.
5. Many positions will appear.
6. Find 12 to 15 positions you could do tomorrow.
7. Print all 12 to 15 positions.

8. Take a yellow highlighter (you are now looking for your keywords).

9. Look across each position and begin to see both mandatory and "nice-to-have" requirements.

10. Highlight those words you see repeated (again and again) across the positions.

11. Create a list of the above common qualifications.

12. You now have a list of keywords for that particular job title or position.

By completing the above exercise (for each job position), you will find keywords used by employers in posting job positions in the ATS.

For example, if you are targeting jobs in *customer service*, you will have a list that may contain words like customer communications, retention, customer satisfaction, order processing, sales administration, metrics, inter-company communications, and call center experience.

If you are targeting the *hospitality field*, your key words would be completely different and might include back-of-the-house operations, catering, kitchen management, food and beverage, vendor negotiation, inventory planning and control, menu development, and serving size.

You may also be able to pick up keywords used in your industry by reviewing the websites of your target companies, reading their annual reports, and consulting trade magazines.

There is no guarantee when it comes to your résumé being read. But you can increase the likelihood by ensuring that your résumé and cover letter include as many of the keywords listed in a job description as possible. It is appropriate for you to slightly modify your résumé each time you apply for a position to make sure the keywords for a particular position are included.

Creating a résumé that is rich in keywords is the difference between being noticed by a human recruiter or not. Be sure to skillfully incorporate keywords throughout your cover letter and résumé (featuring keywords in sections of your career summary and areas of expertise). By doing this, you increase the likelihood of your résumé reaching a decision maker and making your skills and abilities easier to understand.

Stop Employers in Their Tracks

Finding a job boils down to having companies' hiring authorities pause and pay attention to your job application, cover letter, and résumé. You want to break through the clutter of the hundreds of résumés sent for each position posted. The key to doing this is creating easy-to-read, technology friendly documents. Building brand *You* creates a distinct impression of thoughtfulness, professionalism, and qualification; it also communicates the brand you are creating. It establishes a unique imprint. In many cases, the visually friendly, direct information will cause decision makers to pause, slow down, think, and take the time to process the presentation of your brand as it applies to the needs of their companies.

Problem Action Result (PAR) Statements

PAR statements help to drive your résumé, cover letter, and even conversations you have with a potential employer. They are individual sound bites portraying:

- Real-life problems you've had on the job
- How you resolved the problem
- Quantifiable, measurable results

The easiest way to pinpoint PAR statements is to create a form. The first column is labeled *Problem*; second column, *Action*; and third, *Result*. Use this exercise to help remember the major on-the-job problems you have solved and what occurred as a result.

Use keywords throughout your PAR statements to increase the chances that your résumé will actually be read by a human being. Remember that PAR statements are just what employers want to see when looking to find the right person for a job. They will be impressed and better understand your transferable skills.

In addition, potential employers will begin to understand how you think and how you solve problems. Be sure to use PAR statements throughout your communication strategy. This will establish your marketability.

PAR statements document your proven and practical decision making and resolution skills. An example is given in the chart below.

PROBLEM	ACTION	RESULT
Incoming foreign delegation w/interpreters Unknown business traditions	Familiarize hierarchy; business traditions; culture; cuisine	Delegation/culture respected; successful meetings and meals; future business partners

CHECKLIST

CHAPTER 12—Keywords: The Hidden Language of the Internet

Are you pulling together brand y*ou?* Do you:

_____ Know your transferrable skills and experiences.

_____ Know your important keywords.

_____ Support your achievements with PAR statements.

_____ What are your hidden keywords?

_____ Do you understand how an ATS works?

_____ Have you utilized Indeed.com or SimplyHired.com to search for 12 to 15 positions you know you could do tomorrow?

Have you:

_____ Printed 12 to 15 positions and identified how many of those mandatory requirements are similar?

_____ Highlighted common requirements?

_____ Utilized the "white space" on your cover letter with your keywords?

_____ Recognized and set up a PAR statement for each bulleted point accomplishment in your résumé?

13

Channeling the Power of the Internet

I am always amazed at the number of people attending my Job Search Boot Camp Seminars™ who assume that 80 to 90 percent of all successful job searches come from postings on the Internet. They are shocked when I tell them the odds of finding a job on the Internet range between 7 to 20 percent. But what if I shared with you a strategy that members of Professionals In Transition® have told me increases their Internet job application response rate by over 50 percent? Although online job postings seem almost limitless, the actual chance of getting an online job is small. This takes into consideration that many companies mandate an online application before the hiring process begins.

My definition of using the Internet as a source to successfully find a job includes:

- Saw the position online.
- Applied for the position.
- Initial interview for the position.
- Additional interviews (until an employment offer is made).
- Negotiated salary.
- Got the job.

Do not spend the majority of your time job search on the Internet. Allocate your time by limiting online applications to no more than 20 percent of your job searching day. Regardless of the actual Internet percentages,

80 percent of all jobs are found through in-person or online networking. This is particularly important if you are geographically bound to a particular city by choice.

The bottom line is that you should concentrate the majority of your time on networking. Budget your time on other sources for potential jobs.

Automate Online Job Searching with Job Aggregators

There is no need to spend endless hours of drudgery on the Internet when you can automate your job search by using job aggregators like www .simplyhired.com or www.indeed.com (see Chapter 12, "Keywords: The Hidden Language of the Internet"). In less than five minutes, you can set up a profile that will do the work for you. Although there are differences between the various job aggregators, you can usually create a profile with properties including:

- Your résumé
- Keywords
- Job title
- Location (radius from your home zip code)
- Age of the job posting (within the past day, week, or month)
- Salary requirements
- Type of job (full time, part time, internship, etc.)

You can then choose how often you want to be notified of these positions via your business email. By automating the process, you eliminate temptations to open other links or stories not related to your job search that appear when you "surf the net."

How accurate are job aggregators? Recently, I compared positions listed on www.simplyhired.com with positions on www.indeed.com using the same search parameters. By using identical job search criteria. I found a 98 percent overlap—that means, 98 of every 100 positions that I reviewed appeared on both sites. Duplicate positions appear because job aggregators pull from the same sources throughout the Internet. Simply choose the job listings you want and apply online.

You can certainly monitor your target companies from day to day for new positions, but new listings will also show up in your job aggregators' profile. You can also follow your target companies on LinkedIn (see Chapter 17, "Social Networking"). Regardless of how you learn about newly posted positions and submit an application online, remember this is only the beginning. When a position is posted online, you and 500 of your closest friends can hit "apply" at the same time.

Internet Black Holes

Even when you do everything right, there is a good chance your application may fall into the black hole of either a job board or a company's database of applicants. Your application is not lost. It simply becomes another addition to the company hiring databank. Because of the sheer volume of résumés received, yours could be "parked" and sit unread for weeks or months as other candidates (for whatever reason) are reviewed first. If a recruiter calls asking if you are still available for a position you applied for months earlier, you know that your information has now become an active profile.

Employers can do whatever they want during the hiring process. Why? because they hold all the chips. For reasons of corporate protection, government assistance, Employment Law, or simply having the control of the process, the application process continues to get more complex and consumes a greater amount of time. Remember that when you play their game, you must follow their rules.

Internet black holes are created when response to a position is much higher than anticipated. Even after you have followed the hiring company's rules, your application can still get parked. Many times, it is simply a numbers game. I was told by an HR professional that she instructed her assistant to "turn off" incoming applications after they received 250. However, the company website listed the position for another week, and it remained on a number of other job search websites. When asked why the job posting had not been removed sooner, she said that most outside listings are available for a minimum of 30 days before being deleted.

In addition, she told me that 250 people is a huge number of candidates to review. These candidates, of course, included only those applicants with somewhere between an 80 and 95 percent correlation between qualifications and keywords and pin-pointed accomplishments or experience that met or exceeded requirements and expectations. Only after these 250 candidates were reviewed and interviewed would the company open the floodgates again to pull another 250 applications from the company database. Remaining applications sat on hold, parked in the database. They may or may not ever get read. In addition, some company policies stipulate that only current résumés are reviewed. Therefore, they do not maintain a database of qualified candidates or applications past 30 days.

How to Increase Your Job Application Response Rate by Up to 50 Percent

Wouldn't it be great if there was a way to boost your response rate and avoid as many black holes as possible? Here's how to determine quickly if you have the minimum requirements for a particular job. The fastest way to find out is by using the T-square (see Exhibit 10-3), which is critical to demonstrating how your experience matches up with the requirements of a position. If your experience does not match or exceed 85 to 90 percent of the requirements for the position, save yourself the time and the frustration of applying. The likelihood is high that your on-line application will either get a quick applicant tracking system autoresponse, such as, "thanks for your application, there were other more qualified applicants," or, even worse, nothing.

So how do you increase your response rate by 50 percent?

- Review potential positions generated by your job aggregator profile and compare the requirements with your abilities.
- Choose a position that most closely matches your keywords. (Refer to "Pinpointing Keywords That Are Right for You" in Chapter 12).
- Copy the description of the position from the ad and paste it into a newly opened Word document.

Crafting an Effective Résumé

- Copy the requirements listed in the position (both required and pre-ferred) and paste them into a Word document.
- Now, go through and show how your experiences matches or ex-ceeds the requirements.
- If your experience does not match the requirements, compensate for each requirement listed.
- Make sure that you paraphrase the requirements or use the words exactly as they appear in the ad for the position. These are the UNIQUE KEYWORDS for this position!
- If you match 85 to 90 percent of the unique keywords, format the T-square letter using (Exhibit 10-3) as your template.
- Keep the T-square letter open.
- Open up your resume.
- Copy your resume into the T-Square Letter file.
- Now save the entire document as: Last Name.First.Name.Resume. Company (that you applied to). For instance, if I applied for Profes-sionals In Transition®, I would save the document as: Birkel.Damian .Resume.ProfessionalsInTransition.doc

Why Does This Increase Your Application Response Rate by Up to 50 Percent?

Applicant tracking systems are trained to find applicants by identifying key-words. These keywords are part of a profile that describes the position and its requirements. Pinpointing the correct key words on your résumé is ex-tremely important. But, you can juice up your résumé by combining it with your T-square letter, as the letter includes the exclusive keywords the com-pany used to describe the position for which you are applying.

By creating one *super* document with a cover letter that contains the distinctive keywords for that unique position, your response rate will go through the roof! Instead of wasting time rewriting your résumé extensively each time you apply for a position, you are concentrating on meeting or exceeding the needs of the employer.

You save time because you only apply for the positions for which you really meet the requirements. As an added bonus, you spend quality time concentrating on finding people whom you know or people you know who may work for the company to which you just applied for a position.

Avoid Getting Lost in the Shuffle

A strong follow through makes the difference between getting noticed and being overlooked. A great way to follow up is to find out if there is somebody you know or if one of your contacts knows someone who currently works for your target company. This allows you to connect with a real person at the company. You may be able to establish a rapport with this person, who could advocate for you from inside. By taking this step, you differentiate yourself from the majority of job seekers who wait passively at home for a response. Think about it. Who would you hire? A person you or your employee knows or a complete stranger? Making a personal connection with a person in the company can make the difference between your application being proactively reviewed or parked.

For instance, I purposely "gave" my résumé for a merchandise manager's position to several people I had previously worked with: one was given to a director at the company; a second was given to a sales representative; and a third was sent with my cover letter and application to the company's HR department. Several weeks later I received a call from the HR director, who said: "I don't know how you did it, but your résumé crossed my desk three times on the same day. This may or may not be the right position for you, but we figured anybody who could engineer this feat we had to meet." It was pure luck; there was no way I could have timed the résumés to arrive the way they did. But by having inside connections, my résumé was viewed by three different individuals and matched to a potential job opening. I did interview for the job, but did not get it.

Another proven way to follow up is to look in your www.linkedin .com connections to see if someone you know works for the company and can make that inside connection. There is also an advanced feature on www.simplyhired.com that (if you grant permission) will go through your LinkedIn contacts and match the positions you select with a person you already know or others you may not know who work at the company and are members of LinkedIn. This gives you the opportunity to contact a real person who works at the company with the job opening, and see if that person may be able to help you.

CHECKLIST

Chapter 13—Channeling the Power of the Internet

Internet positions account for less than 20 percent of all successful job searches.

Do you know:

____   How to channel the Internet?

____   How to automate your job search (and save time)?

____   About the Internet black hole?

Do you:

____   Feel lost in the shuffle?

____   Understand how to avoid getting lost in the black hole of the Internet?

Have you:

____   Created your free business only email and added all job related correspondance to it (i.e. T-square cover letters, resumes, etc.)?

____   Set up your profiles on either simplyhired.com or indeed.com to start recieving job listings?

____   Started to build your LinkedIn profile?

____   Created your list of target companies?

____   Researched your target companies?

____   Followed your target companies on LinkedIn?

14

Creating Internet-Friendly Documents

Have you ever had the highly aggravating experience of almost completing a job application and then being instructed to cut and paste your résumé into that little box at the end of an internet application? If so, you may find that after hitting that paste button your document does populate that tiny field. Instead, your beautiful résumé has morphed through the Internet and become your worst nightmare.

Isn't there an easier way? Yes, however, there is no universal type of document that computers will read 100 percent of the time. Nothing is guaranteed, especially when sending documents from your desktop across the Internet to a hiring company. But you can get closer by saving your document twice: once-as a Word.doc file and then-as a Text.txt file. To convert your Word résumé (.doc or .docx) to a text résumé (.txt), perform the following steps:

1. Name your document.
2. Save as .Doc (defaults to Word).
3. Save again—Look for the drop down arrow (⬇),which shows all formatting styles in which your document can be saved.
4. Scroll down the list and choose plain text.
5. Save as .Txt.
6. A grey box will pop up stating you will lose all formatting, pictures, and objects.
7. Click okay.

Don't panic; it will look garbled. Remember you still have your original Word document on file. All you have done is create a new document in a .txt format which removes the format parameters that Word automatically sets. You will need to reformat the document into a readable outline. Note that the type has also changed to what looks like an old-fashioned typewriter font.

In formatting your document, instead of using a standard bullet (an option in Word), use a tilde (~) located on the left of your keyboard above the tab key or, alternatively, an asterisk (*), which you insert by pressing Shift 8. Once your reformatting is complete, save your document as a .txt file. Text documents hold their formatting parameters and rarely get jumbled.

When you apply for a job and are given the opportunity to copy and paste your résumé, the steps are as simple as:

1. Open your .txt document.
2. Select all.
3. Select copy and then move your cursor to the top of the application's little box.
4. Click and paste. (Your résumé will appear in the box correctly formatted.)

Create your résumé and cover letter separately as .txt documents. Why? Because you will want to customize each cover letter to match the unique requirements (listed in the job posting). However, once you adapt your résumé to a .txt document, you will be able to use it every time you apply for a position. The .txt file will maintain the document's format every time you paste it into that little box. You need to do this because some companies only accept .txt documents. You will know that this is one such company when a box appears at the end of your application that usually states: "paste your résumé here."

For presentation, you may want to combine your cover letter and résumé into one Word document for email and attachment purposes. WORD does have a more finished appearance and looks better when printed. Remember to preview your document for correct pagination, business formatting, and ease of reading before sending.

You have probably heard or seen the term ASCII file. ASCII is an acronym for **American Standard Code for Information Interchange.** The .txt document is an ASCII compliant document, which means the document only "has characters used on a typewriter keyboard. ASCII files can be sent and received by email as attachments . . . but are limited to using only 128 characters."

You can't save a résumé or any other document as an ASCII document. There are many options you *can* choose when saving a file, including various versions of Word (.doc and docx.), .txt, .PDF, OpenDocument Text, Works 6-9, and other formats, but not ASCII.

The bottom line is that most user understand the standard Word package. Save your cover letter and résumé as both a Word document (.doc) and a text document (.txt). If a special format is requested, your documents can be saved in a PDF format by purchasing Adobe software or using Word 2010 or 2013 edition, but special software is required to make the conversion.

CHECKLIST

Chapter 14—Crafting an Effective Résumé

Are you:

____ Using the .txt format to combine your cover letter and résumé when submitting documents electronically?

____ Have you ensured that your .txt résumé is in a readable format?

____ Are you following up with an employer/company after sending an electronic résumé?

The Power of Networking

CHECKLIST

_____ Reexamine your Marketing Plan **(YOU = BRAND).**

_____ Understand informational interviewing; send thank-you notes.

_____ Reallocate "new" work time schedule (electronic time).

_____ Develop/track target lists—companies; people.

_____ Establish LinkedIn profile.

_____ Network.

_____ Connect with unemployed support groups.

_____ Volunteer in community.

_____ Communicate.

_____ Understand referral interviewing; send thank-you notes.

_____ Persistence—one day at a time.

         _____ Build momentum through trial and error.

         _____ Small victories/small rewards.

15

The Visible Job Market

Less than 20 percent of all jobs come from the visible job market. Although the percentages within the visible job market may change from year to year, the overall percentage remains at 20 percent. Regardless of the type of technology used to post a job opening, the range of visible jobs remain consistent. The number of available positions job seekers can view remains the same year in and year out; only the posting channel changes. These channels include:

- Job boards (e.g., www.monster.com)
- Job aggregators (e.g., www.simplyhired.com or rival www.indeed.com)
- Social media (e.g., facebook.com, linked.com, twitter.com)
- Company websites
- Newspapers
- Trade magazines
- Job fairs
- Other emerging media, where everyone can see a posted position

Focus on Activities That Pay Off

Since you know that less than 20 percent of all jobs are filled from the visible job market, you should allocate your time accordingly. Continue to job search on the Internet, of course, but significantly reduce your time by automating your job search using the job aggregators mentioned above and in earlier chapters.

Automating your online job search will reduce distractions and eliminate the hop scotch phenomenon that occurs when you "hop" from page to page and website to website. At the end of the day, you will be astonished at just how far you have strayed from your job search. It's far easier to become sidetracked to non-job related websites (background noise) than to focus on your job search. Discipline yourself to fight the urge to waste the day doing low-impact, trivial activities that do not move you forward. The more you automate this part of your job search, the better. Concentrate instead on high-leverage activities, including:

- Calling a minimum of five people daily
- Sending five to ten letters of approach requesting informational interviews
- (see Chapter 16, "In-Person Networking")
- Participating in at least three informational interviews per week
- Researching potential jobs and companies
- Following up on potential leads
- Following your target companies (online and in print)
- Reading your local business newspaper, paying special attention to job promotions that may translate into position openings and companies or key employees profiled by the paper (everyone likes recognition; a congratulatory note could lead to an informational interview)
- Improving your skill set
- Participating in online discussion groups
- Attending support group meetings
- Going to Chamber of Commerce events
- Volunteering
- Exercising daily (essential for reducing stress, maintaining your energy)

Building Job Search Momentum Over Time

Although networking will be discussed Chapter 16, "In-Person Networking" and Chapter 17, "Social Networking," it is important for you to understand the "bell curve" of job search momentum (see Exhibit 15-1). For your

Exhibit 15-1 The Job Search Momentum Curve

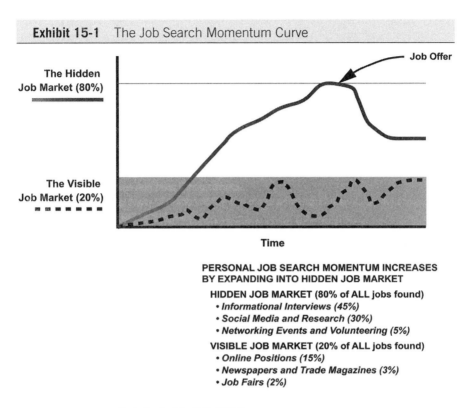

PERSONAL JOB SEARCH MOMENTUM INCREASES
BY EXPANDING INTO HIDDEN JOB MARKET

HIDDEN JOB MARKET (80% of ALL jobs found)
- *Informational Interviews (45%)*
- *Social Media and Research (30%)*
- *Networking Events and Volunteering (5%)*

VISIBLE JOB MARKET (20% of ALL jobs found)
- *Online Positions (15%)*
- *Newspapers and Trade Magazines (3%)*
- *Job Fairs (2%)*

Illustration by John Reidy ©2013

job search to pick up energy and momentum, you need to invest from five to eight hours a day in the activities itemized in the checklists in this book.

There is no easy way to job search. Success won't happen overnight. Searching is a collection of small tasks put together over time that will eventually lead to your next position. Don't stay chained to your computer all day, every day; plan to be out of the house at least three days a week. As you begin your informational interviews and other networking activities, your job search momentum will gradually increase. From an overall time perspective, you want to budget your time as follows:

- Informational interviews (45 percent)
- Searching social media sites and performing research (30 percent of your time)

- Pursuing online positions and other sections of the visible job market (20 percent)
- Networking events (5 percent)

During the first thirty to sixty days of your job search, you will create a résumé, get feedback, incorporate that feedback, and develop all other components of your communication package. This includes your bridge statement, career summary, business cards, 30-second commercial, your résumé and cover letters, and your letter of approach for informational interviews. It takes time to create and revise these documents and then become comfortable using them. While you are developing the execution portion of your marketing plan, you will also be doing extensive research to pinpoint target companies and potential contacts within those companies. If your job search goes like mine, the first month is full of humiliation, error, and frustration, but it gets better, although not necessarily easier.

During the next sixty days of your job search, you should begin to learn how to network. By this time, you will have worked your way through the stages of shock and denial and some of the anger. It's important to have your anger under control before you begin to reach out to others (especially if you are lucky enough to be interviewing). Anger is heard in your voice and on the phone and can be seen in your demeanor. Slowly, gradually, you will feel less vulnerable and will gather the courage to make your first series of calls to set up initial informational interviews.

As you automate your online search, you should start to concentrate on spending more time away from the computer and in the community. Volunteer, go out to lunch with former colleagues, reach out to friends and former bosses, and begin to get the word out that you have lost your job.

At some point during your job campaign, you will feel a shift in your momentum. You will gradually become comfortable reaching out to others and asking for their help (not asking for a job!). You may begin to wonder just how long this whole experience is going to last, but remember that it only takes one job for you to succeed.

After you land your next position, you may notice that you will continue to get offers to interview. You may even receive job offers for up to six months after you start a new position. This is why there is such a long tail on the bell curve of momentum.

CHECKLIST

Chapter 15—The Visible Job Market

Do you know:

_____ The various channels of the visible job market?

_____ How to automate your online job search and eliminate the Hop Scotch Phenomenon?

_____ Expectations: 30–60–90 days into your job search and its possible long tail?

16

In-Person Networking

In-person networking is the process of making direct one-to-one connections . . . one person at a time. Another way to look at it is that you are building a series of job-search allies much like a spider builds a web. In-person networking allows you to accelerate your reemployment. It's a way for you to cut through the red tape and sit down with knowledgeable professionals who can share insights, make connections happen, provide career feedback, and offer additional personal context that might help you find a job.

Going out and meeting people significantly increases your chance of hearing about job openings, getting interviews, and being in the right place at the right time when a job suddenly becomes available. Goals include:

- Gaining insight or perspective about your industry and the companies in your area.
- Spreading the word that you are actively available in the job market.
- Improving your interview and rapport building skills.
- Receiving personal introductions to other key decision makers in your community.
- Establishing ongoing advocates for your current job search and career future.

How to Start the In-Person Networking Process

Select three well-respected members of your community whom you know well and can trust. There are a number of reasons for this:

- They will have high leverage with other members of your community.
- Their good name will open doors you might never find on your own.
- They will help increase the personal effectiveness of your interviewing by enabling you to connect and establish a "top-of-mind" reputation with decision makers. You want them to think of you *first* as future positions arise.
- Lending their good reputation and connections to your job search will empower and prequalify you, as well as add legitimacy to your job search efforts.
- They will be willing to further use their network of decision makers in your area (as you move forward in your job search).

When it comes to building your in-person network relationships, if you don't ask, you will not get help. In-person networking is interactive and occurs during business meetings, informational interviewing, going for coffee or lunch (to gather information), and other gatherings where you are among people of the community. For example, when you are volunteering, you are helping others while making your presence known. In-person networking begins with and ripples out from your primary contacts. Use Exhibit 16-1 as your worksheet to build your networking contact list.

Finding Primary Contacts

You don't have to have friends who are rich or famous or who are related to Donald Trump or Warren Buffett. Anybody you know who makes a living through or with people is a potential candidate for a primary contact. Primary contacts don't have to be connected to your industry. They could be your priest, minister, rabbi, accountant, banker, broker, lawyer, dentist, baker, doctor, florist, mechanic, car dealer, beautician, hair dresser, barber, tax planner, favorite restaurant proprietor, or any other small business owner whom you may know (and *knows and likes you)*. They are the great connectors within your local community. Their livelihood depends on repeat business, a great reputation, and a strong customer base. Don't be embarrassed or afraid to ask for their help. You may have invested resources in them by doing business with them through the years. Asking for a modest

Exhibit 16-1   Networking Contact List

Everybody has contacts. Life would be impossible without them. Your existing contact network may not contain decision makers in your career field, but a few carefully selected people from this page will be useful as initial contacts on which to build your own career contact network.

Former Employers	Past Associates	Professional Association Members
Family/Friends/Relatives	Neighbors	Business Owners
Salespeople	Barber/Beautician	Bankers
Lawyers/Accountants	Financial Planner/ Consultants	Doctors/Dentists
Insurance/Property Agents	Clergy	Church Family
Club Members	Hobby/Common Interest Group Members	People Met While Traveling
Civic Leaders/Politicians	Informational Contacts	School and College Friends

Others:

return on your investment is a perfectly fair expectation on your part. This is not the time to be timid or shy. Business is both *personal* and *reciprocal*. Many people stop patronizing a business or change churches because of an unjustified embarrassment or shame after asking for help and counseling. Whatever the reason, you should not be embarrassed or ashamed.

Leverage is a combination of getting help from people you already know and learning whom else to meet with to gather additional information. Most of the time, you will be calling someone at the recommendation of a known acquaintance—making a "warm call" instead of a cold call. The person you're calling should be far more likely to meet with you because of the acquaintance you mutually share.

Primary contacts will ask you what type of people you want to network with. You should be looking to network with people who are a minimum of two levels above your current position. You do this for a number of good reasons:

- Your primary contact would not send you if this person could not help you.
- You will be talking with key decision makers.
- Managers or executives usually have an assistant screening their calls, and assistants work directly with their bosses' calendars.
- They will not feel threatened by your request to talk to them.
- Their view or perspective of the industry is much different than yours.
- More often than not, they will remember what it was like when they were networking into different industries and/or positions.
- The people they refer you to will be at their level, not yours.

Getting the Most from Your Networking

As you begin to work out from you primary contacts, follow this proven formula for networking success:

- Have a finished résumé and cover letter template.
- Develop and be comfortable discussing your career summary.
- Know the companies you're most interested in targeting.

- Know which professionals you want most to meet, and why you want to meet them.
- Ask questions that will further your understanding of critical issues, business conditions, practices, changes and trends within specific industries, particularly as they relate to your area of expertise. Prepare five to ten "Igniter Questions" for this interview.

Sample Igniter Questions about business trends and critical issues are:

- What are some important long-term trends affecting this industry (sector)?
- How do you see these trends affecting marketing strategy (or other functional areas of the business)?
- What are the critical issues facing your industry today?
- What are some important sources of information I could use to keep up to date on this important issue?

Overview of the Networking Process

1. Receive the referral.
2. Mail a letter of approach (see Exhibit 16-2A) in a business-sized, stamped envelope. Or, if your contact is a personal acquaintance, email an abbreviated letter of approach (see Exhibit 16-2B), enlisting all the etiquette of a written letter of approach (as noted below).
3. Follow the golden rules of networking described below.
4. Be patient as you follow up with attempts to schedule the meeting.
5. At the meeting, be sure to ask your igniter questions.
6. Request three additional referrals.
7. Send a thank-you note within three days after the networking meeting.

Letter of Approach

Most business communication is sent via email. Because of the sheer volume of emails, many will sit unread, especially if it comes from someone unknown to the person (or whose name is not recognized). On the other hand, a well-written, folded letter sent through the U.S. mail in a business-sized envelope will stand out and get read.

Exhibit 16-2A Letter of Approach

YOUR NAME
Address
City, State Zip Code
Telephone/Cell
Email Address

9/9/9999

Janet Cooper
Director
Architectural Design Office
RTA Engineering Associates
5512 West Pine Avenue
Akron, OH 44520

Dear Ms. Cooper:

John Sayres suggested that I write you regarding my interest in architectural drafting. He thought you would be a good person for me to contact for some sound career advice.

I am particularly interested in improving construction design and building operations in shopping center complexes. In addition to learning more about your position at RTA engineering, I also hope you would share your perspective on the following questions:
- How did you get started in this industry?
- What do you like the best and the least about your industry?
- How do you see your industry changing over the next 5 to 10 years?
- What qualifications are required for success in your industry?

John mentioned that you are one of the leading experts in this growing field. Would it be possible for us to set up a twenty-minute meeting at a time that is convenient for you? Currently, I am at a crossroads in my career and would appreciate your advice and expertise.

I will contact your office next week to determine if it is appropriate to schedule a time to either talk or meet.

Thank you for your time and interest.

Sincerely,

YOUR NAME

TIPS FOR ALL LETTERS: Sign your name in black or blue ink.
Follow up on telephone calls/contacts as stated.

Exhibit 16-2B   Email Letter of Approach

TO: johnsmith@houston.rr.org

SUBJECT: Advice

Hi John,

How are you? It has been a while since we have talked, and I trust your new position at Seatex is going well. I would like to let you know what's going on with me and my job situation and get some advice from you. Your breadth of knowledge of the chemical industry in this area could provide me with some valuable insights and information.

I have attached a copy of my résumé in Word to refresh your memory on my background and experience. My goal is to find a position as a chemical engineer in a Houston area company.

Please understand that I do not expect you to have or know of a job.

I will call you next week in hope of arranging a time for us to meet.

Best wishes to you and your family,

Phillip Brown
pbrown@houston.rr.org

HINTS:

- *Mention the program you used to create your attachment as well as a cut-and-paste text version in case the person receiving the résumé doesn't have the software to open your résumé attachment. Ensure your format is clean and error free.*
- *Follow through on your statement to contact or call the recipient.*

A well-written letter of approach includes:

- First paragraph, first sentence—the name of the person who referred you.
- First paragraph, second sentence—why this person referred you.
- Second paragraph—a clear statement that you do not expect them to know of or have a job; you are requesting information only.
- Third paragraph—request twenty minutes of their time. Highlight briefly the most important questions you would like to ask.

- Conclusion: "I will follow up with you shortly to arrange a mutually convenient date and time." Don't forget to let the person who referred you know you have sent a letter of approach (in case your new contact speaks with your referee).

Telephone Communications
Effective letters of approach can create a polished and professional first impression. But there's a reason why the postal service is often labeled "snail mail." Telephone, cell phone, or electronic communications can result in a more efficient and quicker response to:

- Setting up meetings
- Confirming information
- Keeping in touch on a regular basis

Telephone communications means the human voice using proper telephone etiquette and techniques. Effective use of the telephone requires thorough preparation. Remember that the primary mode of communication is sound or, more specifically, the spoken word. Preparation, therefore, consists of carefully choosing words, phrases, and sentences relative to your subject, and then planning how to use them for maximum effect.

The major goal of advanced planning is to eliminate wasted time: yours certainly, but more importantly, that of the person you are calling. A well thought-out phone call will sound focused and professional and will duplicate that same professional image you created in your letter of approach. An impactful telephone call will produce a more cooperative response than an off-the-cuff, unprepared call requesting unorganized information.

- Follow these rules to get the most from your telephone communications:
  - Always use the name of the person who referred you.
  - Be prepared to deal with gatekeepers. . . . It is their job to screen calls.
  - Be friendly, but persistent.
  - When telephoning to set a time to meet, always ask if your target has a moment to talk. If not, ask when a better time to call back is.

- Your primary objective is to arrange a face-to-face meeting (twenty minutes).
- Establish a meeting time and place (be creative).
  - Be prepared to do your informational meeting on the phone then and there, if that is your only option.
- Have your calendar available.
- Thank your contact and confirm the agreed-upon meeting details.

Sample Phone Script: Setting Up an Informational Interview

- Use this script as a starting point and modify it to suit your own style and circumstances.
- You have less than 30 seconds to make a positive impression and communicate your purpose.
- To sound confident, stand up while you are talking. Make sure your voice pitch goes down at the end of your sentences. If it goes up, you will sound unsure and tentative.

Greeting and Reference to Referral	Hello (contact's name). (*Referral's name*) recommended I contact you. My name is (first and last name).
Purpose	I am currently researching (industry, function, etc.) and *referral's name* thought you would be an excellent resource for me to consult to find out (information you are seeking). The reason I am interested in this information is. . . .
Reassurance	I want to emphasize that I am gathering information at this time in my job search. I clearly do not expect you to know about any job opportunities. My intent is to benefit from your knowledge and experience in (industry, function, etc.)
Ask for Meeting	Would you be available to meet with me to discuss these issues for twenty minutes sometime next week? Would (e.g., Tuesday morning) be convenient, or is there a better time for you?
Confirm Meeting Location	I will meet you at (time) on (day/date) (in your office) at (location).
Thank You	Thank you for your time. I'm looking forward to talking with you.

The Golden Rules of Networking

Regardless of how badly you want a job, to be successful at in-person informational networking, you must follow the Golden Rules of Networking:

1. Never **ask** contacts for a job.
2. Never **expect** contacts **to have** a job for you.
3. Never **expect** contacts to **know of a job** that would be right for you.

The Golden Rules of Networking are important because

- You immediately let the person "off the hook" in terms of feeling they have any responsibility to provide a job for you.
- By following the rules you can relax and truly learn about the person you have worked so hard to meet.

Networking Success Takes Time

Be patient as you follow up with attempts to schedule a meeting. It is easy to become frustrated when your letter goes unanswered and your follow-up calls unreturned. However, your patience will be rewarded eventually. Each time you meet a contact you build another advocate in your job search. Every referral you receive helps build your credibility, your personal brand, and your knowledge of the job market.

Follow the Rule of 3/30

When it comes to following up on letters of approach, use the Rule of 3/30: *make three contacts every thirty days.* This translates to about one follow-up call every ten days and communicates that you are persistent, but not a pest.

A Week Before the Meeting

- Send a quick email reminder with the Subject: Confirmation. After a brief greeting, confirm the date, time, and location of your meeting in the body of the email.
- If available, provide a meeting agenda with questions you want to ask. If your questions are not prepared at this point, send another email no less than two days before your meeting with your most important questions. Cut, paste, and update your original letter of approach to include your key questions of interest. To prepare for the meeting, review Exhibit 16-3.

Exhibit 16-3 Preparing for a Network Meeting

Know Your Objective

The meeting is scheduled. Now you must prepare for it by determining your objectives in advance. By doing so, you create an agenda and will structure your meeting to maximize your time with each contact. Your objective may be to:

- Identify key players you want to meet, such as decision makers at target companies.
- Brainstorm about your career options.
- Obtain information about the growth or hiring trends of other companies in your industry.
- Brainstorm names of other industry related companies.
- Obtain at least three names of other professionals in your industry.
- Ask contact to call ahead to a potential employer and introduce you and your skills.
- Discuss how your skills may translate to a new but related industry.
- Discover where potentially you may fit in the company.

Possible Questions to Ask–

- Would you look at my target list and tell me if you have any contacts in these companies?
- What do you see as the future trends in this industry?
- Can you name other companies that might be interested in someone with my background?
- Do you know the names of any good recruiters in my field?
- Do you have any ideas about industry associations or strategies I may not have considered?
- Do you know the names of any industry specific websites I could investigate?
- Are you aware of any companies in the area with openings in my field?
- Can you suggest what other positions might match my skills and background?
- What skills are employers looking for in this particular industry?
- Can you provide me with three to four names of other people who might be willing to speak with me?
- Who do you know who works in (fill in the industry/field or company)?

- Make sure to include your cell phone number in case there are any last minute changes.
- Reemphasize the golden rules of networking.

At the Meeting

- Begin with a quick update regarding the person who referred you.
- Thank the person for seeing you.
- Mention that you plan to take only twenty minutes of their time.

- Restate the golden rules of networking.
- Lead into the agenda for the meeting by referring to your latest email.
- Make sure you have a copy of your résumé and cover letter in a manila folder (to provide only if asked).

Dynamics of Interviewing

You have worked long and hard to get to this point. It has taken weeks or even months to get on the interviewee's schedule. Twenty minutes of quality time will fly by. Realistically, if you get two or three of your questions answered, you have done well.

Watch the Time

If you said you were going to stay for only twenty minutes, at 18 minutes, close your notes and begin to end the interview by saying something like, "This has been a wonderful meeting, I really appreciate the opportunity to learn from you. I mentioned I would only stay for twenty minutes, and I don't mean to take up any more of your time." Stand up, extend your hand, and be prepared to leave. Fully expect to end the interview by saying something like, "I have learned so much today. *Thank you!*" In my experience, the person you are interviewing with often will ask you to sit back down. They usually say something like "Please stay—I know you requested twenty minutes, but I planned an hour for our appointment."

If you are invited to stay, be sure to watch the person's body language. Your extended visit will soon be over. When the person starts to look at his or her watch or the clock on the wall, starts to fidget, or if he or she stops taking notes and suddenly closes the pad, the interview is over.

Ask for Additional Contacts

As you are getting ready to leave, thank them and say, "Before I go, one last quick question, Are there two or three other contacts you might recommend I connect with to have a similar conversation regarding the industry?" This is your rapport check. If they willingly provide additional contacts for you, they have signed on as members of your job search team. Their willing-ness to lend their good reputation to you after just one meeting is a strong indicator of just how successful you were at building rapport. If not, when you write your thank-you note that evening, be sure to mention that you will follow up shortly to see if any other contacts (to network with) came to mind.

Cultivating Connectors

Sometimes you may need additional help to cultivate a connector within the community. Marcus, a trailing spouse, joined PIT® and was trying to network into a major bank here. Chris (a graduate of our program) sug-gested that Marcus consider getting his haircut done by a particular barber whose shop was across the street from the bank. "Even though I don't have much hair to worry about," Chris commented, "my barber has become a great friend over the years and knows everybody in town."

Chris shared that "practically all of the top management of the banks and law firms downtown got their haircuts from Frankie (his barber) and that Frankie had known most of them for many years." He provided Frankie's phone number and suggested Marcus call ahead. Chris recommended he use his name, but that he be prepared for a long wait to get on the much "in-demand" barber's schedule. It took Marcus nearly three weeks to get on Frankie's schedule. After his third haircut, the barber asked him what he did for a living. Marcus shared that he was new in town and was a trailing spouse who had worked for a major bank in his old city. Frankie said, "I know three people you should talk to, but I'm not exactly sure what they do at their banks these days. I've been cutting their hair for the past twenty years since they were young bucks." He handed Marcus the direct dial tele-phone numbers of three men who turned out to be the VP of Advertising, the Director of Marketing, and a Senior VP of Finance for several well-established banks. Less than two months later, Marcus was employed as a manager at one of the banks.

Why is this true story so important? Because Frankie prequalified Marcus by providing a link to key decision makers at the bank who had been his customers for years. He didn't know what their positions were, but he thought they might be able to help Marcus in some way. After a series of very successful interviews, Marcus was confident a job offer was forthcoming. However, because of a hiring freeze, everything came to a grounding halt.

When an assistant manager became very ill, Marcus was hired (in a temporary position) to help fill that gap. This position opened without warning and, because of the sensitive circumstances this position, would never have been advertised. An unfortunate circumstance created an immediate need, and Marcus was there. Even though this was a temporary assignment, the unexpected opening gave Marcus the opportunity to demonstrate his abilities, which eventually led to a permanent position.

In his CD series, *Lead the Field,* Earl Nightingale comments, "*Luck is when opportunity meets preparedness.*" Was Marcus in the right place at the right time? Of course. But there was no way for him or the bank to anticipate the sudden need that arose. Once Frankie provided the names of his customers, it was up to Marcus to follow up on the leads. Frankie's relationship got Marcus through the banks' doors, but Marcus had to prove his worth going forward.

As you move through the networking process, you may begin to hear the same names mentioned. The more often you hear them, the greater your sense of urgency should become to go see them. No one, regardless of how high up they are, is off limits as long as you can get a referral to him or her. Successful people *know* successful people.

Always Send a Thank-You Note

It is human nature to want to feel appreciated. When someone has extended you the courtesy of referring you to a contact or reserving time to talk with you regarding an informational interview, you should always follow up with a short, business toned thank-you note—simple, to the point, and promptly sent to the individual (see Exhibit 16-4).

Depending on the nature of the informational interview (artsy or creative in nature versus manufacturing or laborious), your thank-you note

Follow up each networking meeting or phone call by sending a thank you letter or email within one to two days of the meeting. The header, font, point size, and paper should be the same as is used in your résumé.

YOUR NAME
Address, City, State Zip Code
Telephone w/Area Code   Email Address

9/99/9999

Ms. Belinda Thigpen
Crescent City Investments, Inc.
3619 Poydras Blvd.
New Orleans, LA 70115

Dear Ms. Thigpen:

Thank you so much for taking the time to meet with me yesterday and provide information that already has proved valuable in my job exploration efforts. As a result of your leads, I have arranged two meetings, one with the Sales Director at Whitney National and the other with a Vice President of Prudential Insurance Agency.

I found your perspectives on the financial services industry to be informative. The incisive questions you asked will help me think through the career decisions I face.

Above all, I appreciate the personal support you have shown in my current endeavor. I will certainly keep you posted on the progress of my search.

Thank you again for your time and consideration.

Sincerely,

YOUR NAME

can be handwritten or typed in a business format and then mailed. It is common, convenient, and acceptable to email a thank-you note, but be sure all parties in the informational interview are copied. Remember, however, that the volume of email received may delay the reading of your good intentions and may be viewed as much less personal.

CHECKLIST

Chapter 16—In-Person Networking

_____   Send a letter of approach.
_____   Send email reminders before your meeting.
_____   Understand the dynamics of an effective informational interview.
_____   Establish rapport.
_____   Listen actively, and take notes.
_____   Be enthusiastic.
_____   Watch the time—close on time.
_____   Be flexible and observant.
_____   Watch for nonverbal communication cues.
_____   Send a thank-you note.

17

Social Networking

*P*C *Magazine* defines social networking as: "A website that provides a virtual community for people to share (their) interest in a particular topic or to increase their circle of acquaintances. . . . Facebook is the leading personal site, and LinkedIn is the leading business site."[1]

Social Networking and Your Job Search

Time is of the essence during your job search. Social networking is not an opportunity for you to invest untold hours of your limited job search time trying to master a new website that you have never used before (unless it is one of the five key *types* below). If you are already familiar with a particular social media, keep using it for your job search, but not for games or idle chat.

When teaching, I always suggest a "narrow-and-deep" approach to social networking as the most efficient use of your time. It is far more effective to have a deep knowledge of a few social websites than to have shallow knowledge of a wide variety of sites. By concentrating on a few select social websites, you will be able to:

- Learn them more quickly.
- Use them more effectively.
- Coordinate them to create a job search electronic umbrella.

I would recommend the following social networking sites as *must haves* for your job search (even if you have to learn them):

- LinkedIn.com (often referred to as the business Facebook)
- SimplyHired.com or Indeed.com (job aggregators that streamline your online job search by using keywords based on a profile you create to funnel specialized jobs emailed to you)
- Skype.com (allows free "computer-to-computer" calling and conferencing)
- Google.com or Google+ (a web search engine that with its "+" upgrade integrates *existing* Google services, including use of its current search engine, YouTube, Gmail, and calendar, to include newer components of Circles, Huddle, Hangouts, and Sparks)
- Facebook.com (using its newly released job board)

LinkedIn

LinkedIn is an online business directory of professionals and companies you can use for job searching, networking, research, following target companies, and connecting with people you have worked with or may have known in some other business relationship.

- You begin by creating a LinkedIn profile which serves as a mini-résumé. This will give you an immediate Internet presence and, in my experience, your LinkedIn presence will always be listed first when your name is searched on the web.
- Once your profile has been established, business associates/friends can add a recommendation for you regarding your professional reputation and/or skills. Recommendations can contribute to a positive online image that can impact future hiring decisions.
- LinkedIn will also allow you to search for other professionals, which comes in very handy when preparing for job interviews or networking meetings.
- If you're geographically bound to an area by choice, LinkedIn has the ability to focus on a particular position you may be seeking. LinkedIn will call up positions posted within a specified parameter that you set and list people whom you know or are known to work for the company where a job is posted. You can learn more at the LinkedIn.com help center.

How to do it: Log in to your LinkedIn account; then log into your SimplyHired account. When you click on positions listed in SimplyHired, it will show you people already registered at LinkedIn whom you know or others who work in the company and belong to LinkedIn. The listing will be in the right-hand column with the headline, "Who Do I Know?"

• You can also join LinkedIn groups and participate in conversations that are *topic driven*, further increasing your online visibility.

I recommend reading a great series of articles on LinkedIn written by Allison Doyle at http://jobsearch.about.com/od/networking/a/linkedin2.htm

Often, recruiters will contact you in a short email, which indicates that they have reviewed your profile and that you meet the mandatory requirements of a position they are currently trying to fill. Usually, several more emails will follow; these may lead to an initial telephone screening interview to determine if the recruiting process will move to a higher level with you.[2]

Indeed.com and SimplyHired.com

Job search aggregators are huge time savers and simple to use. They make very efficient use of your time. A job aggregator is like a job-finding vacuum cleaner; it scours results from company career pages, online newspapers, recruiter sites, and trade magazines. It then sucks them all together and drops them onto one site for your review. Once you set up a personal profile, it will send the jobs to your email for free.[3]

You will know that the job aggregator you choose is doing its job when you see duplicates of the position posted across multiple websites. Be careful to only post once for each position, regardless of how many times it may appear. The top two aggregators are Indeed.com and Simply Hired.com. I recommend using one or both.

Remember that job aggregators are dependent on the profiles you build. The profiles are built on the keywords you use. Be sure to periodically check industry specific job boards (like Dice.com for Information Technology or SalesGravy.com for Sales to ensure that you stay on top of emerging trends, have the correct names of positions, and use keywords that are current to positions being posted.

Skype®

Skype® is widely known as a software application (now owned by Microsoft) that allows you to make free or low-cost calls across the Internet to other Skype users, cell phones, and VoIP lines. If you are job searching, setting up a Skype account will enable you to do informational interviews (with out-of-town businesses) and also be able to confidently conduct video interviewing (if requested by a potential employer).

But Skype® is about more than just making free calls from your computer. With Skype®, you can send and receive instant messages, collaborate and share documents, and share desktops.[4]

Google

Google.com is a search engine designed to find information quickly and efficiently from multiple online resources.[5] For a complete picture on how to use Google®, I would recommend reading *Search Engine Land's Guide to Google* available at http://searchengineland.com/guide/google. If you have never used Google before, start with http://searchengineland.com/guide/how-to-use-google-to-search

A Google + account will also allow you to:

- Create a professional job *search-only* email address that should contain your first name separated by a period and last name if available (I had to settle for birkeldamian@gmail.com). This email address should appear on your résumé and all professional correspondence.
- In addition, you can upload from your computer all documents you may be using in your job search. Copying documents from your laptop to your Google+ account is a snap.
  How to do it: Sign into your account, find the document you want to upload, click on the file. It is then added to your Google+ account.
- Additional features include a calendar, the ability to pull contacts from other computers, and the ability to access other search engine

email accounts. You will also see links to your calendar and your documents.

Facebook®

In addition to the many things Facebook® has provided to over 1 billion users, it has recently launched a Social Jobs application in partnership with the U.S. Department of Labor, the National Association of Colleges and Employers, the Direct Employers Association, and the National Association of State Workforce Agencies. The app has job listings from other online job boards, such as BranchOut, DirectEmployers Association, Work4Labs, Jobvite, and Monster.com. Right now, users can browse through more than 1.7 million openings.

Like many job search engines, Facebook's Social Jobs app allows users to search for jobs by keyword, job category, subcategory, and location. Clicking on a particular job in the app brings up the details on the Facebook page of the service through which it's listed. There, users are able to learn more about the posting and apply if interested.[6]

For more information on how to use this Facebook app, see https://www.facebook.com/socialjobs/app_417814418282098

Remember that Facebook is used both socially and professionally; LinkedIn is strictly for business. There have been cases where people have lost jobs because of the content of updates posted on Facebook, and employers are being sued by employees and job candidates for demanding Facebook passwords/profiles.[7]

Job Seekers Beware   ABC News reports: "It's become standard practice for employers and schools to peruse potential applicants' Facebook profiles. But in some cases, they are going even further: Some have demanded applicants hand over their passwords so they can view individual's restricted profiles. . . ." It's an invasion of privacy for private employers to insist on looking at people's private Facebook pages as a condition of employment or consideration in an application process," said Catherine Crump, an American Civil Liberties Union attorney, on the ACLU's website. "People are entitled to their private lives."[8]

Be careful what you say on Facebook® and the pictures you upload. More than one interview has been canceled as a result of poorly managed Facebook pages. My cousin is the Director of Engineering, Career Development, for a major university in Kentucky. He has seen numerous examples of students who were crossed off a final interview list on the day of an interview because of his or her Facebook page contents.

Focus on Getting Results

When it comes to job searching, concentrate on the critical few websites (20 percent) that produce the greatest results. Equally important is to avoid the 80 percent that waste your time. This is an illustration of the Pareto Principle, better known as the 80/20 Rule.[9]

LinkedIn.com   The more you access and use LinkedIn.com, the better you become at using this application. The site allows you to proactively reach out to people who may be able to help you with your job search through informational interviewing, insider information, learning about the culture of your target companies, and providing possible insight to the hiring manager of the positions that you seek.

SimplyHired.com or Indeed.com   Once you have set up your profiles, all you have to do is periodically check your keywords and let these sites do the work for you by having them email jobs to you.

Skype.com   Create your Skype account and use it for follow-up calls. This comes in handy particularly when you are searching outside of your geographic area. If this is the case, you may want to upgrade to the paid service, which will allow you to call landlines as well as cell phones.

Google.com or Google+   Use Google for in-depth research and Google"+" to organize your job search.

Jibber Jobber   Another option which allows you to manage and track relationships, integrate contacts + companies + jobs data, and create and get action item reminders (for follow-up) is www.jibberjobber.com. Choose one or the other—Google+ or JibberJobber. Find more information at: http://www.jibberjobber.com/blog/2012/10/05/top-five-websites-for-job-seekers-5-is-jibberjobber

Facebook.com   Facebook is so widespread and simple to use that its new Social Jobs app should prove to be a valuable tool for job seekers. But when you're using Facebook for your job search, stick to that task; it can be much too easy to start straying off course. There is always time off-hours to check out friends and relatives' posts and photos, as well as put up your own.

Social Networking Is Not as Effective as In-Person Networking

Most job seekers spend too much time on the computer practicing social networking. Valuable hours are wasted that could have been channeled more productively away from the computer. Personal time invested in meeting people and giving back to the community by volunteering are far more productive and rewarding. Time spent nurturing contacts (attending business events, helping others, or participating in informational interviews) are more beneficial than the incredible amount of time required to learn a new social network site from scratch.

The importance of in-person networking as compared to social networking (as it applies to your job search) really hits home when you review *The Multi-Generational Job Search,* a study conducted by Millennial Branding and Beyond.com. The study reveals that all generations spend almost their entire time job searching online instead of offline (person-to-person networking).

Even though 80 percent of all jobs come through the hidden job market and are obtained through relationships established through in-person networking, the study showed that baby boomers spend 96 percent of their job search online, with Gen *Xer* and *Yers* not far behind. Another way to look at this is that only four to five percent of job seekers' time is spent on in-person networking.[10]

There is no one right way to find a job. At Professionals in Transition®, I like to mention at our weekly meeting the importance of "having as many torpedoes in the waters of reemployment as possible." This means you want to have as many torpedoes firing at the same time as possible, such as responding to positions online, attending job fairs, volunteering, attending church, and other public events.

Remember that social networking is just another tool in your reemployment toolbox. Use it wisely.

CHECKLIST

Chapter 17—Social Networking

_____ Do you know what social networking is?

Are you familiar with or do you use:

_____ LinkedIn? (Business social network)

_____ SimplyHired or Indeed? (Job aggregators)

_____ Skype? (Computer-to-computer calling)

_____ Google and Google+? (Search engines)

_____ Facebook? (Job board connector)

Effective Interviewing

CHECKLIST

_____   Know yourself and review your accomplishments.

_____   Dress appropriately, neatly, and conservatively.

_____   Be polite and personable to everyone you encounter.

_____   Avoid showing signs of nervousness.

_____   Listen to the interviewer and get on the same wavelength.

_____   Focus on your accomplishments/experiences.

_____   Demonstrate enthusiasm, interest, and confidence.

_____   Project optimism.

18

The Interview: Types and Styles

While your main goal is to find a job, the first main objective of your job search is to get interviews. Learning how to conduct yourself in all types and styles of interviews is critical to your success. You'll find that the more times you're interviewed, the more adept you'll become at the interviewing process.

Be prepared to be called back for additional interviews as you get closer to a specific job. This is a good sign. Every now and then a person is hired after only one interview, but this is usually for a position on the lower end of the responsibility ladder and is becoming more the exception than the rule. In my experience, I have seen many potential candidates return to a company four or more times after an initial in-person interview and before a final decision is made on whom to hire.

Types of Interviews

You will come across many types of job interviews during your career. What I have learned though is that each company has its own interview process and that process changes depending on the level of the available position.

Screening Interviews

- Screening interviews are usually conducted on the phone and, in most cases, by an outside recruiter. The two primary types of outside recruiters are contingency search firms and retained search firms; both are hired by the company with a job opening.

- *Contingency Search Firms*—These firms only get paid if they find the person who is hired to fill the position. They are seeking candidates with preferred salary ranges of $50K to $80K and generally charge 15 to 30 percent of the starting salary as a fee. Candidates tend to be specialists in specific career fields, such as information technology or logistics. The job opening is released to a number of outside recruiters at the same time (which is why you may get multiple calls from different recruiters). They all compete to find the right candidate to fill the position as quickly as possible.

- *Retained Search Firm*—There is a high likelihood that you will never hear from one of these firms because they are contracted by the company exclusively to find the "right" prestigious candidate. The preferred salary range is $70K and higher. Retained search firms typically charge 30 to 35 percent of the starting salary as a fee (although flat fees are becoming more common). A retained search firm is not in business to find you a job. "Headhunters" rarely recruit from the ranks of the unemployed. In the rare instances I have seen this happen, it has always been on the senior executive level, and the person hired had a strong ongoing business relationship with the headhunter during his or her career.

- *Inside Company Recruiters*—This in-house group of employees is usually housed in the HR department. Their recruiting function generally centers on filling lower level positions traditionally released to outside recruiters.

- In *smaller or start-up companies*, the screening interview is usually conducted by a company's HR representative or by the hiring manager.

Skype/Telephone Interviews

Skype is the largest (and still growing) VoIP service (Voice over Internet Protocol) on the planet. At any given time, more than 5 million people are using Skype to send and receive calls, instant messages, conduct video calls, and even share documents![11]

Usually companies conduct Skype screening interviews for positions that are located at some distance from the candidate's town, saving hundreds of dollars in travel and lodging expenses. In most cases, the candidate will travel to the company only after he or she has made it to the semifinal list of potential hires.

An *automated telephone interview* may be used when a company is hiring many people, such as customer service representatives. You answer the questions presented by choosing from a list of responses (yes/no, multiple choice) and punching in the number corresponding to your choice of response on a telephone keypad.

Regardless of how you earned your screening interview, *the only goal is to get a second interview.* So, be at ease as you interview and concentrate on building rapport. Remember to demonstrate how your abilities meet the requirements of position and communicate how you are part of the solution to the company's needs.

Second Interviews

This interview can be conducted by HR, along with the hiring manager. Questions focus on your ability to do the job and work with the hiring manager and his or her team. Questions will center on:

- The position, company, industry
- Capability, knowledge, and skill to do the job
- Experience and accomplishments
- Ability to "hit the ground running" (being productive with little or no training)
- Adaptability and readiness to blend into the manager's team
- Determining if there are any outside influences that may affect your availability

It is also possible that questions may be asked to see if you would generally "fit" into the company's culture. Intangibles being probed for include:

- Personal likeability
- Chemistry
- Communication skills
- Personal values
- Work ethic and energy level

Technical Interviews

If you are interviewing for a technical position, expect to also be interviewed by a subject expert. This interview may come before your second interview with a hiring manager. Questions will address your knowledge base as listed on your résumé. Prepare to defend your technical talent and explain in detail key accomplishments and abilities. Your advance research should help you determine what type of data system the company uses. Know current industry issues surrounding the type of data system the company currently has and have knowledge of emerging trends (like moving company data to the "cloud").

Approval Interviews

Conducted by the hiring manager's manager, this type of interview focuses on questions surrounding learning potential, handling the physical aspects of the job, and, as in the first interview, your interest in the position, company, and industry, your work ethic and ability to do the job, as well as your skills, knowledge, experience, and accomplishments. However, once you get to this point in the interview process, you pretty much know the company is interested in you.

The "Fit" Interview

In this interview, you meet with potential team members (your peers). If you are interviewing for a management position, you may also meet with workers who would report to you. During this interview, establishing rapport is critical regardless of the level of people you may be interviewing with. They will provide critical feedback (an evaluation) about you once you have left the interview. You can't fake these types of interviews—relax and be yourself.

Psychological Interviews

Many times you will be required to take a personality test, such as Myers-Briggs, Keirsey Temperament Sorter, or Strong Interest Inventory. Depending on the company, an outside psychologist may be called in to analyze your personality test and determine your degree of fit (with company culture) and motivation (see Chapter 8, "Personality Testing").

The best advice in succeeding in psychological interviews is to be yourself. Answer the questions with the first thought that comes to mind. Don't try to "play" to the questions on the test or asked by the psychologist.[12]

The "Blessing" Interview

This usually is a final interview to offer you the position and is conducted by the highest person within the manager's reporting structure. Depending on the level of the position, the manager could be at the highest level. If the position is senior manager or above, a director, general manager, regional manager, CEO, or president may be involved. This interviewing matrix may change based on the size of the company and the level of the position.

Interview Styles

Every interview is different, but there are a number of interview styles you should know about and be prepared to handle. These include:

One-on-One Interviews

At one time, this was the most common interview format. It was you and the interviewer. Members of PIT® tell me that they now encounter fewer one-on-one interviews and more panel interviews.

Person-to-Person Interviews

This "round-robin" approach involves a series of rotating interviews in which you move from person to person. In many cases, each interviewer will rate you after the interview; then, interviewers will share their evaluations and results. This approach takes into consideration different perspectives and interpretations.

Panel Interviews

Often the panel will consist of a broad range of managers and directors from various departments that interact with the position. This process can be very intimidating. Before interview questions begin, give each panel member your business card with the expectation of receiving one in return. That way you will be able to address each person by name and also send thank-you notes after the interview. The best way to handle a panel interview is:

- When responding, look at the person who asked the question.
- If someone is unfriendly or discourteous to you, treat him or her with special respect. Ask questions to prompt him or her to relate with you.
- Monitor the panel with care and diplomacy. If the interview is with a panel of superiors and things begin to go downhill, don't try taking control of the interview process even if needed.

Stress Interviews

Sometimes an interviewer wants to see how you would react under pressure; how you would respond to a stressful situation; or how quick you think on your feet. Interviewers may pretend to be furious, cynical (of your abilities), provocative, and/or challenging. Your goal is to not react to the situation by losing your cool. Instead:

- Stay composed, breathe deeply and slowly, and maintain eye contact.
- Recognize the artificially created scenario for what it is; don't take it personally.
- Remain calm at all times; step into the process and role play.
- Remain on the positive side of the issues presented. Don't get hostile or angry.

Situational Interviews

Questions asked can be about real or hypothetical situations. How would you react or deal with them? Situational interviews are based on questions involving problem solving and the management of harsh problems that may occur in the workplace. The best way to respond is to provide tangible and measurable examples of how you managed a similar situation on the job. That way, you're providing the interviewer with concrete information on how you reacted and handled the situation.[13] Look for questions like:

- What problems have you encountered at work? Describe how you dealt with them.
- Describe a challenge or problem you faced. How did you handle it?
- Describe a time when your workload was heavy. How did you handle it?
- If you know your boss is 100 percent wrong about something, how would you handle it?
- Describe a difficult work situation/project. How did you overcome it?

Behavioral Interviews

Behavioral questions focus on specific examples from past performance as indicators of your future performance. An interviewer often will take many notes. Behavioral questions will be more focused than traditional interview questions, so you need to respond with specific examples of how you handled situations in the workplace. The PAR response works really well for these kinds of questions. The PAR format is one of the best interview strategies for providing quality information to hiring decision makers.[14] Anticipate questions like:

- Give an example of a goal you didn't meet. How did you handle it?
- Describe a stressful situation at work. How did you handle it?
- How do you work effectively under pressure?
- How do you handle a challenge?
- Have you ever made a mistake? How did you handle it?
- Describe a decision you made that was unpopular. How did you implement it?
- Did you every make a risky decision? Why? How did you handle the situation?

Directed Interviews

In some cases, the interviewer may use what appears to be a script. The interviewer maintains strict control of the interview process, limits the time allotted for each question, and asks specific questions. As hard as this can be (in terms of building rapport), strict control of the questions maintains a high degree of consistency in the content and format of each interview.[15] Questions could include:

- What are your long range and short range goals and objectives?
- How would you describe your strengths and weaknesses?
- What qualifications do you have that are relevant to this position?
- In what ways do you think you can contribute to our organization?
- How has your education prepared you for a career in *XYZ*?

Nondirected Interviews

Perhaps the most frustrating interview is the "fly-by-the-seat-of-your-pants" or "go-with-the-flow" style of an inexperienced interviewer. This interview style is not effective, but some people do use it. In some cases, this style can be a deliberate strategy in which the interviewer asks broad and general questions and allows you to control the interview. The most common, nondirected opener is, "Tell me about yourself." When responding, keep in mind that an employer is interested in how your background, education, skills, and personality qualify you for the position (not in your personal history). In your answer, make sure you acknowledge these areas: your education, relevant experience, valuable skills and abilities, and personal characteristics. Practice your answers before you go to an interview. It is vital that you sell yourself and your qualifications.[16]

Practice Makes Perfect

Even if you are not interested in the position, *never turn down an opportunity for a job interview*. It may have been many years since you've had a job interview or perhaps you've never had to do a job interview. Every interview you have will make you more comfortable with the process. If you are like most people, you find that job interviews are far and few between during your job search. However, if you have been doing informational interviews throughout your job search, the time between job interviews won't feel so long. Most people don't know how to network or do very little networking once they are unemployed. This means the only chance they have to practice the critical skill of building rapport is during their job search and while job interviewing. Each time you are given a chance to interview, you'll have an opportunity to practice and build rapport. Every time you interview, the process will get a little easier. Remember, you are always in control of the process. Even if a job offer is made, you don't necessarily have to accept it.

CHECKLIST

Chapter 18—The Interview: Types and Styles

_____ Do you understand the differences between contingency search firms and retained search firms?

_____ Do you understand who company recruiters are and why their numbers are increasing?

_____ Have you considered setting up a Skype account? Do you know how to use it?

_____ Do you know the purpose of a first interview?

_____ Do you know the dynamics and variables of a second interview?

_____ Are you familiar with the many interview types and styles?

19

Informational Interviews

Rapport is a sense of mutual liking, trust, and shared understanding and concern. You should establish rapport the minute you walk into a room. Your strong handshake, the way you carry yourself, sitting straight and poised, the direct eye contact you make throughout an interview—all these are elements of compelling confidence. Your courteous, warm, and friendly manner along with your smile demonstrate a willingness to listen and respond effectively to questions asked. Combine this physical certainty with your positive, proactive nonverbal communications, and you create a convincing impression and establish a presence of strong rapport.

Building Rapport

Building rapport is a learned habit developed long before a job interview and enhanced by traveling the many pathways of networking. Since 87 percent of Americans are by nature shy, most do not know how to network or build rapport. In the 40th edition of *What Color Is Your Parachute?*, Richard Nelson Bolles refers to a European version of networking developed by Daniel Porot, who creates rapport using his PIE methodology:

P—Warm-up interview (practice—sharing of common interests; pleasures; leisure)
I—Informational interview (sharing knowledge; support; referrals)
E—Employment interview

A tried-and-true way to build rapport is by conducting "informational interviews." In a brief informational interview (usually 15 to 20 minutes), you seek information that is of common interest to you and the person you're interviewing with; information about something you enjoy doing or find relaxing. By talking with someone about a common interest, you engage in a "warm-up" conversation while networking with an "expert" about a topic you both have in common. Thus, this simple conversation builds rapport or a connection. If you plan on finding this person through another person in your field of interest and are planning to write them a letter, use Exhibit 16-2A as a template to contact the individual. A couple of warm-up "igniter" questions you might consider asking are:

1—How did you get involved in this (activity)?
2—What do you like most about it? What do you like least?
3—Who else would you suggest I talk with who shares our interest? (This now provides referrals or leads into an area of interest you may consider pursuing.)
4—May I use your name? May I tell a referral that I met with you and you recommended that I speak with him or her?
5—Would you be willing to call (the referral) and let that person know I will be contacting him or her?

You know by the number of referrals you receive how successful you were at building rapport with that individual. Remember that you promised to stay only 15 to 20 minutes. You should begin to close the interview at the 18-minute mark regardless of where you are in the interview (unless, of course, your expert wants to continue talking about the subject).

Small business owners use this method of information gathering to develop their business contacts and support services. A common interest is shared and, by word of mouth, ideas are developed, networking contacts are exchanged, and connections are made.

A member of PIT* remarked how similar the PIE networking methodology was to the 10 Steps of Salesmanship. He pointed out:

- How having a common interest (product) and being able to talk about it (promoting information) gives you the confidence and passion of being a salesperson. (What is salesmanship other than the personality and skill of conversation?)
- How conversation builds rapport; rapport builds trust and respect; and ultimately, customers will not do business with someone they don't like. (In an informational interview, you approach someone whom you believe to be an expert in your field of interest.)
- How talking with an expert in a desired field or activity offers so much insight into likes and dislikes, expands your knowledge and concept of that field or activity, and possibly triggers thoughts of new avenues to consider and develop. (Conversation gives you the opportunity to ask questions relevant to your interest.)
- Through conversation, you develop "a mutual understanding and interest." Informational conversation should be nonstressful and relaxed. You are comfortable asking for referrals (others who share your common interest) and thus your networking tree adds another contact or two!

Informational Interview Benefits

- Provides exposure to meeting new people.
- Builds confidence in talking with people about common interests (developing interviewing skills).
- Provides additional contacts relative to your common interest and builds rapport with contacts (building a network contact list).
- Your developing networking contact list could very well provide the next opportunity for reemployment (courtesy of informational interviewing).

CHECKLIST

Chapter 19—Informational Interviews

_____ If your networking contact is someone you have never met, send a letter.

_____ Follow up by telephone to set a meeting time.

_____ Have a prepared list of questions.

_____ First priority is to build rapport.

_____ Are you conscious of the time? Do not go beyond your requested time.

_____ Conclude the meeting. Have you asked for other contacts?

_____ Follow-up: Thank-you note within one-to-two days after your meeting.

20

The Screening Interview

et's face it—interviewing is stressful! The selection process makes people anxious anyway, and the pressure mounts when you are actually talking to a representative of a potential employer. In most cases, the screening interview will be your first human interaction with an employee of the company or with a "recruiter" (see Chapter 18: "The Interview: Types and Styles"). A screening interview is designed to filter out candidates based on abilities and keywords as matched against the position requirements. The notification that you have an interview means the employer is interested in you. Congratulations!

This means you have also survived the scrutiny of the company's applicant software system designed to highlight any hole in your résumé, including:

- Gaps in your employment history
- Information that seems suspicious
- Too high a salary demand for the company

The screening interview also enables the company to check your qualifications, how you communicate, and if you are in its salary range. The person conducting the screening interview is looking to determine:

- If you meet basic qualifications for the position.
- Have the experience needed to do the job.
- Appear to match the company's workplace environment.
- Are within the salary range of the position.

How to Handle a Screening Interview

A screening interview may be conducted over the telephone or in person. Remember, it is designed to save company time and eliminate questionable candidates as quickly as possible. In today's "employer market," most selection screening interviews are with an HR recruiter or an outside resource company hired to sift through the massive number of incoming résumés. The recruiter knows you are qualified to do the job, as your résumé has indicated that. But, while you may have the skills to perform the tasks required by the job, the question remains as to whether you can interact well with management and/or coworkers without disrupting the functionality of the department. A bad "fit" could ultimately be costly and affect the company's bottom line. Many experts feel this "smooth continuity" can be determined within the first several minutes of an interview.

The screener's goal is to find a reason to eliminate you. Telephone screeners call when it is convenient for them, not you. However, if the phone rings and you are caught off guard, politely ask if you can reschedule the call so you have an opportunity to prepare. This is not the time to shoot from the hip. Even if you can only delay the call for an hour, you will have time to collect your notes and be better prepared. If the screener insists on going forward, gather your notes (résumé/cover letter, pencil) while heading for a quiet place and follow these simple strategies:

- Stand during the interview. Your tone will sound more proactive and confident.
- Make sure you know the first name, last name, and title, of the person so that you will be able to send a thank-you note.
- Focus on the positives: your accomplishments and credentials.
- Answer questions directly and candidly.

During a screening interview, your aim is to provide accurate information about your qualifications. Be friendly, listen actively, and don't be afraid to ask about the next appropriate steps. You can show your enthusiasm and personality in later interviews with the person making the hiring decisions.

If asked, do not mention a specific income requirement. Instead, provide a range that would satisfy your needs. Deflect income inquiries with responses that show flexibility, such as, "I am confident that I will be able to fit within the salary range for this position."

Your only goal in a screening interview is to get a second interview. Knowing you do not have to make the sale on the first interview can be a huge relief. Instead, concentrate on building rapport. Remember that, "If they like you, they *may* hire you; if they don't, they *won't*." It is a simple way to remember to always keep rapport building in the forefront of interviewing.

Preparedness Is Always Key

How well you are organized when preparing for an interview is critical. It means having relevant information at your fingertips. You should always have your notes easily accessible, including:

- Your T-square cover letter. Be prepared to explain, in detail, the abilities you listed as they apply to the requirements of the position.
- Your résumé. Be ready to defend your entire résumé. Remember the screener is trying to figure out your thought process in a brief phone conversation. Frame your answers using the following sentence: The *problem* was _____; the *action* that I took was _____; and the *result* was _____.
- Original company research. Highlight important points usually found in the About Us section of the company's website.
- Any recent developments (since your application). Read the media section, newsroom, and investor areas of the website

If you are able to prepare for a telephone interview or know ahead of time when the screening interview will be, allow plenty of time to set up and be ready.

Position all your notes/documents on a separate table near your desk. To save space, it can be a folding table used only for phone interviews. Consider increasing the size of the font for these documents for easy reading during a telephone interview. You may have to do a little bit of reformatting, but larger type calls attention to important points that you may want to make during the interview. Consider keeping an extra pair of glasses close to your notes so you don't struggle with your notes (your voice will reflect it).

When the phone rings, stand up and answer: "Hello, this is *first name, last name.*" All business phone calls should be answered this way because it:

- Is appropriate business protocol.
- Sounds professional.
- Avoids confusion.
- Identifies you immediately.

Answering the phone in this skilled manner (even on Caller ID) starts the conversation in an even-measured business tone. *Remember to stand up through the entire interview.* You do this because the tone of your voice is different. When you sit, the tone of your voice sounds more casual and relaxed. When you stand, the tone of your voice becomes more proactive and assertive. You might want to hang a picture of a person at eye level above your desk. Be sure to look at it, and pretend it's the person you are talking too.

Have Answers Ready for Typical Questions

Be prepared to answer the following:

- Questions that determine your general level of experience. (Example: How many years of retail management experience do you have?)
- Specific questions that compare your overall abilities with the specific needs of the company (Example: What is it like to manage annual sales over $15 million?)
- Questions that will assess specific areas of your experience as they apply to the needs of the company (Example: Tell me about your experience with point-of-purchase inventory reorder systems.)
- Questions to determine your level of education (Example: Describe your educational background and experience as it applies to this position.)
- Salary Questions: *Be Careful! Do not reveal your salary requirements.* Once you reveal your salary requirements, you lose all negotiation

power. (Example: Not to limit you or commit you to a certain dollar figure, but what's the minimum salary you'd consider right now to accept another position? You might say something like, "I would rather postpone salary discussion until we are further along in the process. I am confident that my salary expectations will fall within the position's salary range. What is that range?")

- Standard background checks. (Example: Are you willing to agree to have a drug test, a criminal background check, references checks, educational background checks, and others as appropriate for this position?)

Once you reach this point in the screening interview, the call will either be terminated (the screener eliminates you) or you move into phase two of the screening interview process. In addition, more probing questions are then asked. These could include:

- What was the size of your previous company in terms of yearly sales?
- What was your typical day? Walk me through it.
- How many employees worked for your company?
- What were the company's primary products and markets?
- How many people reported to you directly?
- What were their titles and responsibilities?
- Why and when did you leave your last job?

After Business Hours—Screening Calls on the Rise

If the screener is the decision maker, there's a high likelihood she will call you after hours after her regular work is done. Remember that even though finding a job is your first priority, to the person screening applicants, filling an open position is just one of many things on a to-do list. Keep your cell phone on and your résumé/notes handy until at least 8:00 PM each working day in case an after-hours screening call is made.

Recently, a student of mine received a screening call from a recruiter at 9:00 PM. Linda was particularly shocked because she had applied for the position more than eight months ago and had had *absolutely* no response. She had just sent a final follow-up email which prompted the call. The late-night screening interview went very well, and Linda was informed a follow-up interview would occur the next week.

Another late night call from a different company soon followed. Three months earlier Linda had applied for a position as a high-level church liaison, but she received no response. She mentioned this in class and another student recognized the decision maker's name. Jeff agreed to fire off an email to him sharing Linda's talents and interest. As a result of Jeff's email, Linda received a telephone screening interview at 8:00 PM, which resulted in a face-to-face interview.

The bottom line is that as the workday lengthens, screening interview calls will continue to be made long after the traditional workday ends. It is something we all have to live with. Recruiters, hiring managers, and others may perceive the unemployed as "on call" and always available. When it comes to screening interviews, it is what it is, and you have to take what you can get.

CHECKLIST

Chapter 20—The Screening Interview

_____ Are you prepared (at any time) for a telephone screening interview?
_____ Remember to be enthusiastic, be confident, and build rapport.
_____ Do you have your résumé and details easily at hand?
_____ Can you provide accurate information relative to your qualifications?
_____ Are you smooth and professional on the telephone?
_____ Do you know how to avoid revealing salary requirements?
_____ Did you ask for a contact name or telephone number for a follow-up plan?

21

The Interview:
Concerns and Questions

Congratulations! You have survived the telephone screening interview! Enjoy your triumph, but now you've got to get ready to walk the uneven road leading to the *possibility* of getting hired by this company. There are many steps ahead. You've got to take the time and prepare the best sales promotion you can—selling yourself in person. This is your chance to demonstrate how your unique differential advantages/abilities (1) *fit* the requirements of the position; (2) *fit* with the type of boss who will be supervising the position; and (3) *fit* within the overall culture of the company.

Three Key Concerns

While there are hundreds of questions you could be asked during a series of job interviews (and you will be asked many of them), the entire interview process boils down to three major concerns:

- Are you qualified for this position? (skills, knowledge, experience, learning potential)
- If we hire you, will you do the job? (work ethic, energy level, willingness, availability)
- Will you fit in our company's culture? (chemistry, values, work style, appearance)

Rosemary Haefner of *CareerBuilders* references a leadership survey conducted between November 9 and December 5, 2011, regarding the interviewing process. She comments, "Employers aren't hiring a list of skills and accomplishments. They are hiring the whole person; their personality; their résumé; their critical thinking; and their creative ability. The impression made during an interview will always be the determining factor in landing a new job."

Effective interviewing involves addressing these key concerns. If you remember nothing else from this chapter, remember the following two statements:

1. *Be the answer to the employer's needs.* Reinforce how your skills match the requirements of the position. Set yourself apart from other candidates by illustrating how your unique qualifications and willingness to do the job will enable you to be *"the fit"* for the job. Establish how your experience complements the job that currently exists in their organization. Be positive. Know yourself, and know your qualifications.

   Caution: As much as you may want the job, you are not "Superman." You cannot be "all things to all people." You are a polished professional qualified to fill the position. Continue to "sell yourself" up until the last minute and then afterward in your thank-you note.

2. *If they like you, they may hire you; if they don't, they surely won't.*— You can be brilliant and have all the necessary qualifications, but you won't be hired if there are any "red flags." If you have a poor work record, a bad reputation, or are known for being a troublemaker in your former job (uncovered by some investigative checking), most companies won't hire you.

Eight Cardinal Rules for Answering Interview Questions

1. Keep it brief; don't talk too much.
2. Listen carefully; Show you are interested.
3. Don't be modest, but don't exaggerate.
4. Don't be arrogant.
5. Talk in concrete terms.

6. Never defend or argue a view during an interview; never interrupt.
7. Make connections for the interviewer; build rapport.
8. If you draw a blank, pause, establish eye contact, smile, and reply, "That is a great question, I need a minute to think about it."

Red-Flag Questions Frequently Asked by an Interviewer

1. Tell me about yourself.

The question "tell me about yourself," is not only a request for information, but also a signal to start the interview. In employer terms—tell me about yourself translates to, "Why are you here and what do you want?" This first question will (in many cases) determine the tone and course of the rest of the interview. At this point, you don't know the interviewer's expectations, problems, or needs. *Proceed with caution.*

Pause, smile, and ask, "What part of my background would you like me to talk about?" Most interviewers will be relieved (knowing that a long autobiography is not forthcoming) and welcome the opportunity to help you make your responses relevant. If you are given the choice, begin with your 30-second commercial. Sound natural and convey your intelligence, enthusiasm, and confidence. Pause, and then ask, "Would you like me to go into more detail?" or "Is there anything in particular you would like me to talk about in greater depth?" Let the interviewer take the lead.

Leave out any weaknesses or failures until specifically asked, and then only as they relate to your professional image. Expressing weaknesses or failures is not an opportunity to sound desperate for a job, to tell of personal or family problems, or share anything else that may be of a private nature. This is a business interview, so keep it professional. Disclosing private matters can sabotage your interview and may create a negative, unspoken response from the interviewer.

2. List three of your strengths.

Link your strengths to real accomplishments or life incidents. Reinforce your strengths through credible examples of tangible, measurable benefits. Highlight skills and strengths directly related to the job you are seeking.

Speak confidently about your experiences and demonstrate how *you are the answer to the employer's needs.* Now is not the time to be modest, but neither do you want to appear arrogant.

3. List three of your weaknesses.

Careful. . . . Probing questions are not asked to gather data. Instead, difficult questions are a request for reassurance. Consider addressing hidden questions most interviewers have, but may not ask: *"Do you work well with others?"* *"Will you fit our corporate culture?"* *"Will you do the job?"* *"Can you accept leadership?"* *"Can you provide leadership?"* Your ability to respond to difficult and probing questions is a reflection of your attitude. If the interviewer continues to probe, illustrate examples of strengths instead of weaknesses.

Responding to a weakness or failure question by saying "I'm a perfectionist at heart" is an automatic deal breaker and has just ended the interviewer's interest in you. Why? Because no one is perfect; everyone makes mistakes.

4. What did you like most and least about your last job?

Respond by saying something like, "I learned many things. It was an important part of my career . . . (choose a few key highlights from your résumé)."

5. How would your boss describe you?

Reinforce your career summary and reflect your key areas of strength through your supervisor's eyes. In my case, I would repeat the last sentence of my career summary and say, "My boss would tell you I have excellent organizational development and business partnering skills gained in day-to-day participation directed at achieving bottom-line results." Never criticize or complain about your boss or coworkers.

6. Why did you leave your last job?

Be honest, professional, and positive in your response. If you were downsized, it is perfectly appropriate to say so. Avoid statements that may sound negative.

7. If you had to live the last ten years of your life over again, what would you do differently?

Start by saying, "I feel good about the decisions I've made during the past ten years and would not change much." Then, reinforce your strengths and say, "And I feel particularly proud about the following key decisions. . . ."

8. What is the biggest mistake you ever made?

Everyone in life makes mistakes. Consider responding by saying, "I usually do not have a problem recognizing, resolving, and then learning from mistakes I have made (big or small)." Share one example of a task where personal initiative and responsibility did not work. Highlight what was learned and what you would do differently in the future. Conclude by saying, "My employers have always been supportive of my efforts."

Remember that no one is perfect!

9. Assuming we hire you, where do you want to be in three years?

An effective response to this question is, "I would first do the job offered to the best of my ability. Eventually I would hope to earn a chance for advancement by significantly increasing my contributions to your company."

10. What are your salary requirements?

Be prepared! Know your salary range before the interview begins. A great resource for salary ranges and other related research is at http://www.salary .com or www.careerbuilder.com, which features a salary calculator. Until you have clarified that the interviewer is satisfied with your ability to do the job and offers you the job, try to postpone responding to this question. If an employer is genuinely interested in hiring you, the interviewer will not be put off by your reluctance to answer. You can politely skirt the salary issue and shift the dynamics of the interview by stating, "I would like to postpone any salary discussion until I have a better understanding of the job we are talking about. Please tell me more." or "Once you have decided I'm right for the job, I will be delighted to talk about salary. I am sure your income structure is a fair one, and I will have no trouble fitting in" (see Chapter 23, "Salary Negotiation").

11. What do you know about our company?

This is where your research comes in. Are you familiar with the company's major products or services? Do you know its mission and internal culture? Do you know the industry's trends? All this information lends to credibility.

12. Why do you want to work for us?

Pause and think about what you want to say. Then direct your answer directly to the needs of the company. A definite mistake is centering the answer to this question around "You"—what you can do for the company or how the company will benefit from your being an employee.

13. What accomplishment gave you the greatest satisfaction?

Is this a strength you should elaborate on; an interest you work at outside of work; or a skill you have developed to the point of consistently being called upon to perform? This is the opportunity to toot your horn (in moderation).

If certain questions arise as you conduct informational interviews, there is an excellent chance that the same questions will be asked during an actual job interview. Learn to recognize "red-flag questions" and develop a strategy to address them comfortably. Know the questions and practice the answers so you sound smooth and confident. A lack of self-confidence is a turnoff for employers.

Sensitive Questions

In a perfect world, interview questions should be related to the position and your willingness and ability to do the job. Occasionally, an interviewer asks questions that solicit information about you that could potentially be used in a discriminatory way. Questions regarding the following items are not legal; these items should never be included on your résumé. A recruiter once told me she is legally required to discard résumés with volunteered affirmative action information because of potential legal problems. Such questions might ask about:

- Age; gender
- Race; ethnicity
- Marital status; family/children
- Physical attributes (this does not include any handicaps or disabilities)
- Inclusion of a picture
- Religious or political affiliation

Practicing how you would handle these kinds of questions will help you respond professionally if questions are asked in an interview situation (or even on an application).

Remember:

- Many interviewers are not trained in interviewing. They may not know which questions to avoid or which questions are illegal.
- Inappropriate questions are often unintentional. Such questions may be based on perceived relevance rather than legality, with no malice intended.
- Use your common sense and react objectively, not defensively.

If you are presented with potentially discriminatory questions:

- Maintain eye contact. Remain cool, calm, and professional.
- Be aware of your body language. Consciously manage your nonverbal reactions to remain as neutral as possible.
- Ask for clarification on how the question might relate to the responsibilities of the job.
- Evaluate what the interviewer is really seeking. For example, questions about children may relate to potential absenteeism or questions regarding working with minorities may relate to customer base, work group, or how you evaluate people.
- Answer in a neutral, positive way.
- Express concrete facts and ideas. Avoid feelings.

Sample Questions to Ask an Interviewer

An interview should not be a one-way street. Be ready with questions of your own to ask the interviewer that will help you gather relevant information about the job you're interviewing for and the company itself. How many people have held this position in the past few years? How have they advanced? Questions might include:

- What skills and characteristics are you looking for in the person you hire?
- Is the department team oriented? Are employees independent or is the workforce highly structured?
- How would you describe your management style?
- How does the company handle professional development?
- Where do you see the future of the company? Of the department? Of this position?
- Do you encourage new ideas?
- Is there a regular review process? How are the employees judged?
- What stage of the hiring process are you in? What is the next step? What is your time line?
- Describe a typical day for someone in this position.
- What is the most urgent short term issue that needs to be addressed?
- What are your department's long-term goals?

References

Sooner or later you will be asked to provide references. *Do not* offer references until asked. Reference checks are made to:

- Assure that you told the truth about yourself.
- Get a feeling for how you work with others.
- Pick up otherwise undisclosed information, either positive or negative.

Today, many employers are very careful about sharing information due to the chance of a lawsuit. Often, a company will only provide a job title and dates of employment when asked about a former employee.

Select Appropriate References

Choose people who know you in a work setting—managers, peers, and subordinates. They are your best references. Customers or vendors are also good choices, along with well-known political, community, or business leaders, educators, or professional trade association experts. Do not use neighbors, relatives, and doctors. All references should know you well enough to speak objectively and in some detail about your skills, strengths, and personal characteristics.

Prepare Your References to Help You

Typically, you are asked for three references. You will need to have several more references just in case. Prepare a reference list to give a prospective employer using the following format:

Reference List

- Your name at the top of the page
- For each of your references, provide:
  - Name
  - Phone numbers
  - Current and former titles
  - Address
  - Relationship to you (former manager, subordinate, coworker, etc.)
  - Current company

Help Your References Help You

1. Ask first.
   - Always ask a person to act as a reference before you provide his or her name to an employer.
2. Prepare your reference.
   - Provide a copy of your résumé to the person.
   - Develop a one-page summary, including your career objective and reason for leaving your last job, strengths, weaknesses, and work and management style. Then, review it with him or her.
3. Call your reference when you give his or her name to an employer.
   - Provide details about the prospective position and what you have to offer.
   - Share your excitement and enthusiasm.

4. Ask for feedback after your reference has been contacted.
   - What types of questions were asked?
   - What topics were covered?
   - What concerns were raised?
5. Thank your reference!

Now that you have made it through the screening interview and the face-to-face interview, it is worth your time to write a short thank-you note or letter, via email for expediency or by post for a lasting impression of manners (see Exhibit 21-1). This may very well be the factor that seals the job selection in your favor. It is important that your thank-you note or letter be written within 24 hours of your interview, so the interviewer will remember to connect your face and presence with your thank-you note.

Exhibit 21-1. Thank-You Letter

YOUR NAME
Address, City, State Zip Code
Telephone / Cell
Email Address

9/9/9999

Thomas F. Harris, Director
Human Resources Department
BYCOASTAL PRODUCTS, INC.
7229 Lakewood Drive
Denver, CO 82170

Dear Mr. Harris:

Thank you for the opportunity to interview with you last Thursday afternoon for the marketing position available with your company. I appreciate your hospitality. I enjoyed meeting you and the members of your staff.

The interview convinced me of how compatible my background, interests, and skills are with the goals of ByCoastal Products. My prior marketing experience with the Department of Commerce has prepared me to take a major role in developing both domestic and international marketing

(continues)

Exhibit 21-1 *(continued)*

strategies. I am confident that my work would result in increased market shares for ByCoastal Products in the rapidly expanding Pacific Rim.

Regarding your interest in new product promotion, David Garrett at the Department of Commerce is the person to contact. His telephone number is 999.999.9999. I talked with Dave this morning and expressed your interest in this program, indicating that you may be contacting him.

Again, thank you. I look forward to seeing you and your staff again soon.

Sincerely,

YOUR NAME

CHECKLIST

Chapter 21—The Interview: Concerns and Questions

_____	Are you what the employer is looking for?
_____	Remember to be enthusiastic, be confident, and build rapport.
_____	Can you expand confidently on your 30-second commercial speech?
_____	Are you familiar with red flag questions?
_____	Do you know how to respond to them?
_____	Have you practiced answers to sensitive questions (that may be illegal to ask)?
_____	Do you have a list of references, if asked?
_____	Are your references comfortable recommending you?

22

Strategies to Ace an Interview

We have all been guilty of judging a book by its cover, but it is often that critical first impression that makes the difference. People who create an initial image of success are considered more intelligent and competent—and they often earn more money. In addition to the suggestions in previous chapters, here are more things you can do to ace an interview.

Dress for Success

Regardless of the ongoing trend in America of companies adopting a "business-casual" work environment, when it comes to a job interview you want to look your very best. According to Kim Zoller at *Image Dynamics*, 55 percent of someone's perception of you is based on how you look.[1]

You will want to dress well and conservatively. Women or men cannot go wrong with a classic, tailored, high-quality suit in traditional solid colors, such as navy, gray, or any other neutral. You can complement the suit with conservative jewelry and accessories.

It is far better to be overdressed (looking like a penguin at a formal ball) than to wear a t-shirt and flip flops or tennis shoes. If you are overdressed, you can easily relax your interview attire by taking off your tie and suit jacket. If, on the other hand, you go into the interview wearing flip flops and tennis shoes (and to your surprise, find everyone in $600 penguin suits), there is no hope of recovering.

When people ask me how to dress for an interview, I always suggest they dress as if they were going to a religious service or a wedding. Business "formal" assures you will pass the image test in the milliseconds before the interview even begins. Your grooming must be impeccable, and your hairstyle clean, neat, and fashionable.

Do not use heavily scented perfume or aftershave/cologne. Fragrance is a personal preference and can be offensive or trigger allergies in others. You can't go wrong if you simply smell fresh and recently showered. You don't want to leave a negative impression because of the way you smelled.

Take the time to drive to the location of the interview the day before it is scheduled and park your car near enough to observe people as they come in and out of the building. Are they smiling? Or are they hunched over? Are they all wearing $600 suits or jeans and tennis shoes? Find out as much as you can about the style of the people or company who will be interviewing you so you convey the impression that you are a good fit for their culture.

A seasoned interviewer will begin to make judgments about you in the nanoseconds of first sight—even before you shake hands and formally meet. Interviewers size you up, from head to toe. Nanosecond observations include:

- Style of your hair
- Quality, color, and coordination of your apparel
- Type of watch or jewelry worn
- Brand of shoes, and whether they are polished

Nanosecond observations are converted into first impression conclusions almost like an intuitive sixth sense.

Presenting a Professional Image

During your job search, you should look professional at all times. You never know whom you may meet and where. Looking professional does not mean you have to look like everyone else. It is critical, however, to dress for your audience. Every style sends a message and that message should address the industry you are targeting, as well as reflect your personal taste.

For Men

- For most industries, opt for a conservatively tailored, well-made suit. Quality is the key—the suit should fit you perfectly.
- Shirt color preferences are white or light blue. Pink or pin-striped shirts are generally not good selections for a first interview, although in more casual or fashion-conscious industries, they would be acceptable choices. A man's tie is the most important part of his outfit. It is his only chance to add contrast and his own sense of style. A good quality tie can totally enhance a man's suit, so it is well worth the investment. Ideally, your tie should contrast with your suit. Avoid wearing a solid tie with a solid color suit.
- Accessories are an important part of your total look. Shoes and belts should be good quality leather and should match in color. Black, cordovan, or brown are the best color choices. Either laced shoes or slip-ons are appropriate. Socks should be worn high enough so that your legs don't show when you sit or cross them. Interviewers react negatively to flashy buckles and ornaments on shoes, so these should be kept as simple as possible. Follow the same rule with belts. Briefcases and portfolios should be leather.
- Jewelry should be kept simple and limited to either a wedding or signet ring. Although tie clips and cufflinks may be appropriate after you have the job, they are sometimes thought to be inappropriate, as are pocket handkerchiefs, which depending on the culture of the company, can be viewed as too flashy. Watches should also be simple — just a dial face and leather band. Heavy watches with a lot of functions should be left at home.
- Your grooming must be flawless. There is no question that the clean shaven look is safest for a businessman. It makes most men look younger, cleaner, and more efficient. In addition, many people have negative reactions to mustaches and full beards. There are always exceptions, of course. A neat, well-trimmed mustache may make a man look more mature and in control. A full beard still falls into the high-risk area in corporate America. In more creative professions, such as college teaching, architecture, psychology and advertising, beards are acceptable.

- Your hairstyle should be neat and up to date. A good stylist is key to giving you a cut that is easy to care for as well as flattering to your facial features.

For Women

- The best choice of dress for a woman is a good-quality suit (whether skirt and jacket or tailored pants). Wear a conservative suit in a style that compliments your figure. Neutral solid colors, such as taupe, navy, gray, or black, are safe. Other colors are acceptable, but stay away from bright colors.
- Blouses can be worn in almost any color that is flattering to your skin tone. Silk, cotton, and silk look-alikes are good fabric choices. Choose collars that compliment your jacket lapel and face shape. For example, if you have a long, thin face, avoid a neckline that repeats the shape of your face. Try to express your own sense of style in blouses.
- Accessories are very important and can easily upgrade an outfit. Choose leather pumps in classic styles for interviewing. Heel heights vary with fashion, but a moderate heel height is always a good bet. Flats may be too informal and an excessively high heel is not businesslike. Belts should generally match your shoes and, again, should be conservative in style. Belts are good finishing pieces and serve to tie your outfit together, although scarves used as belts can be too informal.
- Handbags and briefcases are items people always notice. Quality is imperative, so pay attention to craftsmanship and materials. One word of caution—don't carry both a handbag and a briefcase to an interview. It looks clumsy and requires too much juggling. Make sure whatever you are carrying closes easily and is not overly full. Better yet, save the briefcase until you have the job.
- Jewelry should be kept simple. Fine jewelry is always acceptable, but good quality costume jewelry can also add versatility to your wardrobe. Appropriate jewelry might include simple earrings (no dangles), a string of pearls, a chain or conservative necklace, a watch,

and no more than two rings. Any bracelet or necklace that tends to jangle is distracting and should be avoided.

It's Showtime!
You only have one chance to make a good impression. Be sure to arrive early and use the visitors' restroom before you announce your presence. Look in the mirror. Now is the time to readjust your tie, brush your hair, check your makeup, pull up your pantyhose or complete any finishing touches necessary to prepare and compose yourself for the interview.

Of equal importance—and a matter of visual impression—is that you should definitely not chew gum. An interviewer watching gum roll around in your mouth as you talk or listen does not get a good impression of you. Get rid of it, and use a breath mint that dissolves quickly.

While much has to do with the way you look during this split-second process, never underestimate the power of your *body language.* The old adage, "It's not what you say, it's how you say it," still holds true even, if you're not talking. You need to successfully connect, both verbally and nonverbally, with the person or panel interviewing you.[2]

The Approach
When you are ready, make your presence known at the front desk no earlier than ten minutes before your scheduled interview. Most likely, you'll be escorted to the interview location or asked to wait in a receiving area. Don't become impatient if you feel "parked." Last-minute crises happen, delays occur, meetings run over, and schedules change unannounced. Use this time to review your notes about the company and reexamine some of the interview questions you believe have a high likelihood of being asked to answer. (It also doesn't hurt to take a look around and try to get a "feel" for the environment and the people you observe.)

Handshake
Remember—nanosecond observations and first impression conclusions were made in the first 30 seconds of visual sight—before the interviewer extends his or her hand to greet you. Immediately establish eye contact, smile, and

shake the person's hand firmly. Be careful. Don't squeeze the person's hand. Hurting an interviewer with painful arthritis with a linebacker's handshake is the last thing you want to do. Of 2,000 bosses interviewed by Patrick Ritter, *Info-Graphic Overview: What You Wish You'd Known Before Your Job Interview*, 26 percent viewed a weak handshake as a common nonverbal mistake at a job interview (see Exhibit 22-1).

Exhibit 22-1   The Job Interview

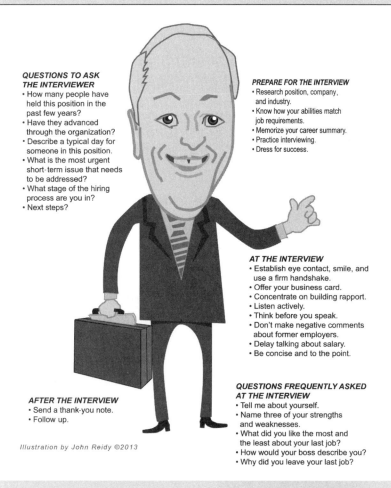

QUESTIONS TO ASK THE INTERVIEWER
- How many people have held this position in the past few years?
- Have they advanced through the organization?
- Describe a typical day for someone in this position.
- What is the most urgent short-term issue that needs to be addressed?
- What stage of the hiring process are you in?
- Next steps?

PREPARE FOR THE INTERVIEW
- Research position, company, and industry.
- Know how your abilities match job requirements.
- Memorize your career summary.
- Practice interviewing.
- Dress for success.

AT THE INTERVIEW
- Establish eye contact, smile, and use a firm handshake.
- Offer your business card.
- Concentrate on building rapport.
- Listen actively.
- Think before you speak.
- Don't make negative comments about former employers.
- Delay talking about salary.
- Be concise and to the point.

AFTER THE INTERVIEW
- Send a thank-you note.
- Follow up.

QUESTIONS FREQUENTLY ASKED AT THE INTERVIEW
- Tell me about yourself.
- Name three of your strengths and weaknesses.
- What did you like the most and the least about your last job?
- How would your boss describe you?
- Why did you leave your last job?

Illustration by John Reidy ©2013

Eye Contact

Maintain eye contact. It is important in our culture to look at the person to whom you are speaking approximately 80 percent of the time. Americans place a high value on eye contact and generally interpret it as a gesture of trust and confidence. During an interview, make eye contact when you are talking—particularly when making an important point—as well as when you are listening. Nodding is another gesture of support and agreement. It is complementary to eye contact.

Again, Patrick Ritter notes that 67 percent of the 2000 bosses viewed failure to make eye contact as a critical nonverbal mistake made during a job interview (see Exhibit 22-2).

Body Temperature

If your hands tend to sweat, they may create a damp, slimy feel, so be sure to wipe them off with a handkerchief, tissue, or paper towel before you shake another person's hand. Alternatively, if you are cold blooded, prior to the interview run warm water onto a towel and hold it in your hands to bring up the warmth in your palm.

Nonverbal Body Language—Do's

- Demonstrate from the start that you are in sync with the interviewer by following that person's body language. Sit up, establish eye contact, smile, and lean a little forward in your chair. Carefully observe how the interviewer sits, and then subtly match the body angle. This will demonstrate your interest and project confidence and willingness to be the answer to the employer's needs.
- Listen actively and ask permission to take notes. Reinforce your interest throughout the interview by making positive gestures. Keeping eye contact, tilting your head, smiling, and nodding are positive gestures of a good listener, all critical attributes to display confidence during an interview.[3]
- When you are in a panel interview, make sure you establish immediate eye contact with the person who is asking a question. Establish eye contact, one by one, with each panel member for a moment. Then,

Exhibit 22-2   What You Wish You'd Known Before Your Job Interview

From a Survey of 2,000 Bosses

Common Nonverbal Mistakes Made at a Job Interview
- 21 percent: playing with hair or touching face
- 47 percent: having little or no knowledge of the company
- 67 percent: failure to make eye contact
- 38 percent: lack of smile
- 33 percent: poor posture
- 21 percent: crossing arms over their chest
- 9 percent: using too many hand gestures
- 26 percent: handshake that is too weak
- 33 percent: fidgeting too much

Things That Have an Impact on First Impression

Statistics show that when meeting new people the impact is:

- 7 percent: From what they actually say
- 38 percent: The quality of voice, grammar, and overall confidence
- 55 percent: The way we dress, act, and walk through the door

Clothes

Is how you dress important? 65 percent of bosses said clothes could be a deciding factor between two similar candidates. So, how should you look during an interview? Seventy percent of employers claim they don't want applicants to be fashionable or trendy. You may also want to stay away from bright colors since they are typically a turnoff.

Top Ten Most Common Mistakes Made at a Job Interview
1. Overexplaining why you lost your last job.
2. Conveying that you're not over it.
3. Lacking humor, warmth, or personality.
4. Not showing enough interest or enthusiasm.
5. Inadequate research about a potential employer.
6. Concentrating too much on what you want.
7. Trying to be all things to all people.
8. "Winging" the interview.
9. Failing to set yourself apart from other candidates.
10. Failing to ask for the job.

Most Common Interview Tips
1. Learn about the organization.
2. Have a specific job in mind.
3. Review your qualifications for the job.
4. Be ready to briefly describe your experience.

Five questions most likely to be asked

1. Tell me about your experience at _____.
2. Why do you want to work for us?
3. What do you know about our company?
4. Why did you leave your last job?

About the Author

Patrick Ritter is a thirty-year veteran of management consulting in America, Asia, and Europe who discovered a love of writing many years ago. Four novels, two kid's books, numerous newspaper columns, magazine and web articles later, he still loves writing ... and learning.

return eye contact to the questioner. Address the person by name, and then answer the question. Briefly pan the room to see if you can pick up on the nonverbal reactions of both the questioner and panel members.

- Be flexible. Even during an interview, things can happen that require the interviewer's immediate attention. Show your understanding by indicating your willingness to step outside the office while the incident is being handled. Your tact and ability to respond effectively when a business crisis happens will be remembered and will go a long way in establishing rapport.
- SMILE!

Nonverbal Body Language—Don'ts

- Don't speak too quickly. Match the other person's speech rate. A person's speed of speaking reveals the rate at which the brain can consciously analyze information. Speak at the same rate or slightly slower than the other person and mirror that person's inflection and intonation. Studies show that people describe feeling "pressured" when someone speaks faster than they do.[4]
- If you are rocking back in your chair, shaking your foot, fidgeting too much, or scratching your ... anything, you will be perceived as the type of person who can't stay focused, if even for just a few minutes. It's not a game of charades, it's a job interview.[5]

- Don't drum or steeple your fingers. This implies arrogance and impatience.
- Don't touch your face. Studies show when someone is concealing information or lying, face touching frequency increases dramatically because of an increase in blood pressure in the face, especially inside the nose. If you have an itchy nose, people who don't know this are likely to think you're lying.
- Don't let your arms drop inside the arms of the chair. Keep your elbows out. Sitting with your elbows on the armrest of a chair is perceived as a position of power and conveys a strong, upright image. Humble, defeated individuals let their arms drop inside the arms of the chair; keeping their elbows close to the body to protect themselves. They are perceived as fearful or negative, so avoid sitting like this.[6]
- Don't clench your fists or your jaw even if it helps control the natural anxiety you may feel when interviewing. The interviewer, however, may view this as hostile or uncooperative.
- Don't cross your arms at your chest. This tells the interviewer you are upset or defensive. For more information on negative body language, see Exhibit 22-3.

Exhibit 22-3.   Negative Body Language: Did You Know?

Applicant's Body Language	Typical Interpretation
Avoiding eye contact	Evasive, indifferent, insecure, passive, nervous
Scratching the head	Bewildered
Biting the lip	Nervous, fearful, anxious
Tapping feet	Nervous
Folding arms	Angry, disagreeing, defensive, disapproving
Raising eyebrows	Disbelieving, surprised
Narrowing eyes	Resentful, angry
Flaring nostrils	Frustrated
Wringing hands	Anxious, nervous
Shifting in seat	Restless, bored, apprehensive

Above all, remember your positive attitude is key and that positive nonverbal behavior naturally results from positive attitude. As 55 percent of your credibility is based on communication, your body language can convey a stronger message than your words. Proper body language is critical in business situations. Your entrance, handshake and eye contact all make a first impression.

CHECKLIST

Chapter 22—Strategies to Ace an Interview

_____   Have you dressed for success?
_____   Have you presented a "professional image"?
         What about that first impression?
         _____   The handshake.
         _____   The eye contact.
         Are you conscious of your nonverbal body language?
         _____   Do's.
         _____   Don'ts.
         _____   Negative body language.

23

The Salary Negotiation Process

Most job searching books you read approach salary negotiation from a defensive position. The opposite is true. It is your proactive ability to establish and maintain rapport through the entire hiring process that becomes so critical. If the hiring and subsequent salary negotiation process does not "flow" with both parties feeling good along the way, there is little chance you will be hired.

After your first several interviews, your goal is to help the process flow forward toward the job offer phase. But, until you actually get a job offer, you should only talk about what you can bring and do for the company. Continue to reinforce how your abilities match the employer's needs. Understand that the process or "flow" can be interrupted by business circumstances and become fragmented—or even chaotic. Bridge this time by sending short emails to the people with whom you interviewed. You can also make contact by mailing newspaper or magazine articles on topics of interest to the individuals you have met.

Salary Goals

When it comes to hiring a candidate, HR's job is to hire you at the lowest possible price within the competitive salary range for your area of expertise. Your job is to negotiate the highest salary possible.

The minute you disclose your salary goal, all significant salary negotiation ends. Even worse, revealing your desired salary creates a maximum
salary ceiling in the eyes of the employer. Hiring decision makers will make
a mental note of your requirement and offer you a much lower amount at
the start of the formal negotiations. In my experience, I have found little to
no way to negotiate around this figure.

Keep in mind that revealing your salary demands too early could also inadvertently create any of the following scenarios with a salary decision maker:

- The salary you provide is too low. The employer may begin to question your ability to do the job. Your stated wages are far below what
  the company was prepared to pay for the position. This has created
  doubt in the employer's mind that did not exist before.
- Your compensation expectations are too high and the salary decision
  maker(s) become hesitant. This is because you've not yet had the
  chance to demonstrate your added value to the organization, and
  they don't understand why you might be worth it.
- The requested wages are within the company's range, but your bargaining position has become awkward. This is because the company
  knows your salary request falls in its range, but you don't.

Decisions surrounding the hiring of a new employee are highly charged
with emotion. Establishing whether that job candidate will "fit" into a company and if the potential employee "is right" is a combination of sensitivity
and intuition. Experts have confirmed that hiring decisions based on emotions are often very successful after establishing "fit," qualifications, and
willingness to do the job. Building rapport and salary negotiation go hand
in hand together to create the next step of the process, which is effective
salary negotiation.

When to Discuss Salary

It does not matter how many job interviews you have had with a company.
The only way you will know when to address salary concerns is if you are

comfortable enough to ask the direct question, "Do you agree I am the right person for the job?" If the employer's answer is vague or the subject is quickly changed, you will then know it is too early in the process to discuss salary. Fall back and reinforce how your unique abilities meet the needs of the organization and demonstrate how your skill set matches the requirements of the position.

Until you receive agreement from your potential employer that you *are* the right person for the job, *do not* reveal your salary history. If you reveal your salary earlier in the process, you have pretty much eliminated any bargaining power you may have had.

How to Answer the Salary Question

During the course of the interview process, you will be asked about salary. It is the way you answer the question that counts. Keep the tone of your voice conversational and your manner courteous, enthusiastic, and interested. Here are a few key phrases you can use to avoid revealing salary:

- "If you don't mind, I would like to delay any salary discussion until I get a better understanding of the position."
- "I am sure you have a salary range for this position. What is that range?"
- "Money is not my top priority, and I can be quite flexible if I need to be. However, I feel I can bring many things to your company. I would like my salary to be based on my value to you."
- "We are both fair people. I am confident I will fit within your salary structure. How much did you have in mind?"

Mid-career professionals who have been laid off often think they have to accept a lower salary because their industry or job experience isn't a perfect fit for a new position. "You have to get out of the mindset that you're starting over," says Elaine Varelas, managing partner of Keystone Associates, a career-management firm. "However, you will need to convince potential employers why you deserve a salary closer to mid or senior level than entry level. . . . This means considering what your years of work experience will add to the organization and what you can do that will bring in more money today. Because functional skills are easy to pick up but problem-solving ability and business acumen is best honed over time, employers often prefer more seasoned candidates."[1]

One-Sided Negotiation

I recently talked to an HR manager, who works in a mid-size manufacturing plant, about his style of salary negotiation. He told me if a candidate successfully met all of the hiring qualifications, he would be offered an hourly amount on the modest end of what was appropriate for the geographic area they were in. But, if the candidate tried to negotiate, he would close the candidate's folder saying the interview was over and thank the person for their time. If the applicant asked for next appropriate steps, most times the HR manager would respond, "None."

I was shocked at this severe and one sided style of negotiation. When I asked why his style was so unforgiving and brutal, he replied, "It's because I have another 100 people waiting in line who are just as qualified and would be happy to take our hourly rate."

In this one-sided style of negotiation, I can only surmise that both the company and its HR manager had bought into the concept that people who are out of work are surplus, damaged, and devalued inventory. Therefore, when it comes to salary negotiation, such "devalued human inventory" should supposedly accept the lowest possible competitive hourly amount as the pay for this position. Like a computer server, telephone system, and office equipment, some companies see people as "human capital." "Capital is capital—you spend something now in hopes of getting a return on your investment later."[2]

The bottom line is that some companies will present you with a "take-it-or-leave-it" offer. Be very careful about an offer like this. Do not be pressured to make a decision on the spot, and be sure to ask for the offer in writing. Then, remember:

- Give yourself a minimum of 48 hours before you set up another meeting to review your counterproposal. Make sure you have checked the financials of this company, fully understand what you're getting yourself into, and are sure you can live with the offer if you counter-propose.

- Companies will lowball their salary offers and blame the economy. This is not the time to give up. This is where the art of negotiation begins. Sadly, I know of many people who have gotten back into their fields and are working at half of their old salary. *Always negotiate!*

Receiving a Job Offer

When you receive a job offer, take the time to evaluate it carefully, so you are making an educated decision to accept or to reject the offer. The last thing you want to do is to make a hasty decision you will regret later on.

Consider the entire compensation package—salary, benefits, perks, work environment—not just your paycheck. Weigh the pros and cons and take some time to mull over the offer. It is perfectly acceptable to ask the employer for time to think it over.

Money Matters

Money isn't the only consideration, but it is a critical one. Is the offer what you expected? If not, is it a salary you can accept without feeling insulted? Will you be able to pay your bills? If your answer is no, then don't accept the offer—at least not right away. Make sure you are getting paid what you're worth and that you are happy with the compensation. Nobody wants to be in a position where they realize their salary isn't enough, particularly after they have already accepted the offer. If the compensation package isn't what you expected, consider negotiating a salary base with your future employer.

Benefits and Perks

In addition to salary, review the benefits and perks offered. Sometimes the benefit package can be as important as what you get in your paycheck. If you're not sure about the benefits, ask for additional information or clarification. Find out details on health and life insurance coverage, vacation days, sick time, disability, and other benefit programs. Ask how much of the costs of the benefits are covered by the company (in full) and how much you are expected to contribute. If there are a variety of options available, request copies of the plans' descriptions so you can compare benefit packages.

Hours and Travel

Before accepting a job, be sure you are clear on the hours and schedule you will be required to work. Confirm what, if any, travel is involved. If the position requires 45 or 50 hours of work a week and you're used to working 35 hours, consider whether you will have difficulty committing to the schedule. If the nature of the job requires you to be on the road three days a week, be sure you can make that commitment. Also, remember to consider travel time to and from work. Is the commute going to take extra time (one way/round trip)? Will there be tolls or parking fees to cover you are not used to paying?

Flexibility and Company Culture

Many of us, with small children or elderly parents (or other personal considerations), need flexibility in our schedules. Is the ability to work a schedule which isn't a typical forty-hour week in an office important? It is important to feel comfortable in the work environment? One candidate for a customer service job realized she could not accept the position when she was told she had to ask permission to leave her desk to use the restroom (despite a decent salary being offered). Ask if you can spend some time in the office before accepting. Talk to potential coworkers and supervisors if you're not sure if the work environment and culture are a good fit.

Your Personal Circumstances

The bottom line in accepting a job offer is that there really isn't a bottom line. Everyone has different circumstances. What might be the perfect job for you could be an awful job for someone else. Take the time to review the pros and cons. Making a list is always helpful. Listen to your gut. If it's telling you not to take the job, there just might be something there. Don't be afraid of your intuition. Every time that I fought my intuition (especially in accepting a job), I ended up miserable and out of work within a year. Keep in mind that if this isn't the right job for you, it's not the end of the world. The next offer you get might just be perfect match.

It's much easier to turn down an offer than it is to leave a job you have already started. The employer would prefer you decline the job rather than to start the hiring process again a couple of weeks down the road if you don't work out. So, take the time to thoroughly evaluate the offer. Ask questions. Make an educated, informed decision so you feel you, and the company, have made an excellent match.

Salary Negotiation

You are practically there sealing the deal for a new job. You've successfully interviewed and even touched on salary. Now comes the challenging task of managing the "give and take" of the salary discussion. LinkedIn research indicates 42 percent of professionals in the United States, compared to their international counterparts, are not comfortable with negotiating, and 25 percent of the American workforce has never negotiated their salaries. Why are American workers intimidated when it comes to negotiating salary and compensation packages? When buying a new car, do you accept sticker price? When you purchase a new home, do you pay the asking price without negotiating? Both are markets to the highest bidder; so is the employment market, but the employer seems to have the advantage. Negotiating is a necessary life skill you need to develop.

Selena Revzani, author of *PUSHBACK: How Smart Women Ask—and Stand Up—for What They Want,* links the intimidation to inflating the other side's power and limiting or minimizing the job seeker's value. She wrote: "Too many workers are satisfied to accept what is offered to them (based on the employer's philosophy—hire the best for the least) instead of setting their sights high, standing behind their value/request, and firmly (yet respectfully) negotiating optimum compensation and benefits. *On average, most companies leave some wiggle room to negotiate when hiring.*"

Consider these recommendations as you look over the entire position and negotiate the full package of salary and benefits:

1. *What is your salary bottom line?*
    - What is the *least* you could accept?

- What do you *hope* to earn?
- Is there room for future advancement?

Know your list of real needs versus "want to haves" and be prepared to demonstrate what your potential value is to the company. If you agree to a lower salary than your needs require, you reduce your income for the length of time that you are with the company. If your salary setback is significant, you may never be able to catch up to where you once were.

2. *Analyze the company.* Of course, if you have insider information, it can be easier to weigh the value of the available position against the need to fill it. Following the company on LinkedIn is an excellent source for learning about movements within targeted companies.
   - How difficult has it been to find qualified applicants?
   - How long has the position been available?

If the company has had difficulty finding someone with your specialized skills, you will have more leverage in negotiating your terms.

3. *Research your market value.* When you can cite facts and figures, it is impressive. It shows you have done your homework.
   - What are workers with your skills earning in your region of the country?
   - Use salary survey tools online to help identify salary bases in your job field (industry averages as well as geographical demands). Such tools include www.Glassdoor.com, www.Salary.com, and www.Payscale.com

Research positions comparable to yours and find the high/median/low scales for specific jobs. If you are backed into a corner while negotiating and MUST mention salary, offer a figure between the high and median scales. Consider offering a range rather than a firm number; this might prove more advantageous.

Providing a potential employer with a written proposal of your salary request gives you the opportunity to showcase your market value, as well as the quantifiable contributions you are able to offer. It also eliminates the need for the employer to take notes.

4. *Be resourceful and creative.* Don't initiate any salary discussions. Wait for the employer to take that lead. But, once salary discussions begin, you might be able to determine if the actual salary figures are negotiable. If not, being flexible and thinking outside the box may offer favorable alternatives concerning other important features of the compensation package, such as:
   • Education reimbursements
   • Vacation time; work schedule flexibility; travel
   • Overtime; days off
   • Expense accounts; stipends; commuting costs; bonuses; commissions

Remember, anything a company can offer can also be used as a negotiating factor (with a twist).

5. *Don't give in.* When a negotiator hears "No" or encounters resistance, he doesn't shut down. Instead, this usually is an indicator to "start the negotiations." Be prepared with an alternative game plan. Understand the elements of the compensation package and be the first to ask clarifying questions, such as those about future raises or ways to tie pay to performance.
6. *Remember these points in a stubborn job market:*
   • Always be respectful and leave a good impression. Never interrupt, ever.
   • Be patient, yet persistent. Give your potential employer time to think. The negotiator may have to consult upper management or do more research. Assure the person that he or she doesn't have to respond to your counteroffer right away.
   • Look for common details and use them to negotiate.
   • Never burn bridges. Communicate in an open and thorough manner. End your conversation on a light, friendly note. Thank you and small talk may lighten a heavy negotiating session.
   • Don't present challenges or ultimatums.

Summary of the Salary Negotiation Process

- Always begin by being very positive.
- Do not enter into negotiations if you do not really want the job.
- Most offers are negotiable. Few are not.
- Negotiate only after a job has been offered.
- Research and organize your game plan fully before negotiating.
- Know your bottom line before negotiating.
- Never say "yes" or "no" until you are ready to do so.
- Always express appreciation over the job offer first—before you begin to negotiate.
- Start negotiating after you have had time to do your arithmetic and homework.
- Conduct negotiations face to face whenever possible.
- If you have another job offer pending, you may want to ask for additional time to assess and compare the offers (see Exhibit 23-1).
  - Contact the other company or organization and indicate you have received another offer. It is only reasonable to give them an opportunity to make a better offer. But, be careful not to convey to either company the impression that compensation is your only real concern and you're just selling yourself to the highest bidder.
- If necessary, you may wish to ask the company with the pending offer for more time, "I want to be sure this is the right decision for everyone."

Acceptance/Rejection Letters

Whether you are accepting or rejecting a job offer, let the company know your decision in writing. In either cases, be polite, brief, and to the point. Here are sample letters to preview. (see Exhibits 23-2A, 23-2B, and 23-3).

With regards to rejecting a job offer, you will want to stay in good favor with this company. You don't want to create any ill-will so don't get into specifics. You want to be able to build on your contacts for future networking and this employer may have a better offer for you somewhere down the road.[3]

Exhibit 23-1 Job Comparison Form

Job Factors - Company Focus	Previous	Option A	Option B	Comments
Size of Company				
Sales Volume				
Number of Employees				
Profit/Nonprofit				
Product/Service				
Division/Subdivision				
Company Growth History				
Profitability				
Future Growth				
Stability				
Reputation				

Job Factors - Job Focus	Previous	Option A	Option B	Comments
Duties/Responsibilities				
Authority				
Independence				
Challenge				
Job Visibility				
Status (Title)				
History/Previous Incumbent				

Job Factors - Compensation	Previous	Option A	Option B	Comments
Base Salary				
Benefits – Basic Health				
Moving Expenses				
Severance Package				
Outplacement Assistance				

Job Factors - Community Focus	Previous	Option A	Option B	Comments
Schools				
Cultural Activities				
Local Taxes				

Exhibit 23-2A   Letter Accepting a Job (1)

YOUR NAME
Address, City State Zip Code
Telephone / Cell Number
Email Address

9/9/9999

Mr. Joe Birkman, President
SAM HOUSTON LOGISTICS
1800 Southwest Loop South, Suite 1790
Houston, TX 77057

Dear Mr. Birkman:

I would like to take this opportunity to accept and formally thank you for the offer to join Sam Houston Logistics as Vice President of Sales and Marketing reporting directly to you. I understand that the effective date is _____ at an annual salary of $110,000. I also understand that I will be eligible for the 15 percent manager's bonus program based on the results of the objectives you and I will set and agree upon the first week of October.

By way of ensuring that we are clear on the other terms and conditions of our agreement, I have summarized my understanding below:
  - The normal thirty-day waiting period for health insurance coverage will be waived under Sam Houston Logistics' group plan so that all coverage will be effective for me and my dependents from_____.
  - I will be eligible for three weeks vacation this year instead of the standard two weeks.
  - A separate letter will be forthcoming from the Assistant Treasurer confirming the immediate award to me of 5,000 shares of Sam Houston Logistics common stock.
  - An organization change will be effected within the first three months of my employment to move the Marketing Department under the Sales and Marketing Department with the managers of both departments reporting directly to me.

I look forward to working with you and Sam Houston Logistics and plan to meet with you on Tuesday, _____, immediately following the new employee orientation program. In the meantime, please advise if there is any other information required or other matters we need to discuss prior to my start date.

Best Regards,

YOUR NAME

Exhibit 23-2B   Letter Accepting a Job (2)

YOUR NAME
Address, City, State Zip Code
Telephone/Cell Number   Email Address

9/9/9999

Marvin Granite and Stoneworks
1849 Conover Drive
Marvin, WS 15589

Dear Mr. Barnes,

As we discussed on the phone, I am very pleased to accept the position of Advertising Assistant with Marvin Granite and Stoneworks. Thank you for the opportunity. I am eager to make a positive contribution to the company and to work with everyone on the Smithfield team.

As we discussed, my starting salary will be $38,000 and health and life insurance benefits will be provided after thirty days of employment.

I look forward to starting employment on July 1, 9999. If there is any additional information or paperwork you need prior to then, please let me know.

Again, thank you.

YOUR NAME

Exhibit 23-3 Letter Rejecting a Job

YOUR NAME
Address, City, State Zip Code
Telephone/Cell Number   Email Address

9/9/9999

Mr. Tom Gilhooley
Director of Marketing
Address
City, State Zip Code

Dear Mr. Gilhooley:

Thank you very much for offering me the position of Marketing Manager with Hatfield Industries. It was a difficult decision to make, but I have accepted a position with another company.

I sincerely appreciate you taking the time to interview me and to share information on the opportunity and your company.

Again, thank you for your consideration.

YOUR NAME

CHECKLIST

Chapter 23—The Salary Negotiation Process

Remember that the company is interested in you; otherwise, you would not have made it this far. Negotiating is a life skill used every day in obtaining high-end, valuable assets. Your professional image and job are critical assets to you, so approach this salary process with a sense of business certainty.

_____ Have you been successful in avoiding disclosure of your past salary base?

_____ Do you know tactful ways to prevent revealing your past salary base?

_____ Will you remember that once you have been offered a job, take into consideration the entire compensation package (not just the base salary).

_____ Have you polished your negotiating skills?

Be positive and respectful.

Be resourceful.

Be patient, yet persistent.

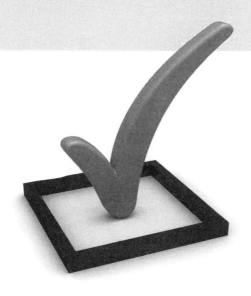

Reemployment: Hit the Ground Running

Congratulations!! You have won the first victory

_____ Reorganize and create your working game plan.

_____ Know your company and its culture.

_____ Maximize your efficiency.

_____ Remember that 85 percent of your success in business is based on your people skills.

_____ Continue your "new hire" orientation and training.

_____ Go the extra mile.

_____ Establish yourself as a team player.

24

Prepared and Ready to Go

CONGRATULATIONS. You've got the job! Now that the euphoria has worn off, you may begin to experience doubt, even before you start. *Relax,* it is perfectly normal. You may be plagued by some of the same questions I had before starting a new job, which included:

- Do I still have what it takes to be successful?
- Am I going to be able to work with my younger manager?
- Will I be able to learn fast enough?
- I've been out of work for so long, what are they really thinking about me?

Learning a new job is a challenge, but there are many things that you can do during your first three months to ensure long lasting *success.* The following series of strategic steps, when combined over the weeks and months ahead, will create a blueprint for long-term success with the company and position that you worked so hard to find.

Prepare Before You Go

Confirm prior to your first day when, where, and whom you will meet. This might be your new boss, someone from HR, or both. Make sure you share cell phone numbers in case there are any delays. Request any special instructions to get into your new office building and have the extension numbers for security in case of any confusion in terms of letting you into the building.

Here are some things you can do to prepare for your new job:

✔ **Ask for Back Copies of the Company Newsletter.** The company news-letter will help you get current with what is going on internally and may give you valuable insight into the company's culture. HR or your new boss should be able to provide this material.

✔ **Pick Up Annual Reports from Previous Years.** Investor Relations should have these available. Annual reports may also be available on-line at your new company's website or at your local library. Use these reports to get a feel for your company's strengths, weaknesses, opportunities, and threats as viewed by upper management.

✔ **Read All Company News Releases (for the past three years).** You can usually find this information on the Media Section of your new com-pany's website. This will give you a feel for the public "face" of the company and how it manages both positive and negative news. It will also provide historical perspective and may potentially avoid embarrass-ment from comments you might inadvertently make as a "newbie."

✔ **Request a Copy of the Company's Long-Range Plan.** You may or may not be able to have access to this prior to starting your job, but it's always a good thing to ask. Even if you have to wait until you officially begin your job, it is well worth the investment of your time to read the plan.

Different organizations may call this plan by different names, but the best long-range plans serve as the foundation of operations for the organi-zation. Even more important to a new employee, reading the long-range plan will provide:

- A framework of how the company plans to conduct business over the next three to five years
- A focus on strategic initiatives
- An overview of both planned areas of company growth and decline

✔ **Conduct Your Own Competitive Analysis.** Nothing is more impres-sive than a new employee who understands the business. Take the time *now* to research the industry and answer the following questions:

- How would you define your new industry?
- What role does the company play within the industry?
- What are the key success factors in the industry and company?
- Is the company growing or shrinking? Why?
- Who are our chief competitors?
- Who are our customers?

✔ **Dress to the Highest Level of Standard Recognized in Your New Workplace.** Be sure to call an HR representative or your new boss for dress code guidance. You want to make a strong impression as people at work begin to form opinions and evaluate you. Dressing to the highest standard communicates that you respect your new company, are professional, and are serious about your work.

✔ **Conduct a Trial Run.** The day before you start your new job, take a trial run. Begin to establish a new daily routine:

- Get up at the same time you will tomorrow.
- Have breakfast, get dressed, start the car, and head to your new workplace.
- Be mindful of the traffic. Time yourself. That way there will be no surprises on your first day.
- On the way home, wash and gas up the car

YOUR FIRST DAY

✔ **Arrive Early.** Arrive at least thirty minutes ahead of your scheduled start time on Day One. Always remember to be kind and patient with the receptionist and any security staff you meet on the way in. They can help you connect with the right people and guide you in the right direction.

✔ **Take Care of Paperwork.** Visit HR, Security, your manager, and anybody else you need to see to fill out necessary forms or other paperwork. Most applications for insurance, retirement, and other benefits will need to be turned in by a certain date. Make sure you know when and to whom they are due. If you're not sure about policies, procedures, or other deadlines; don't be afraid to ask. Be prepared to present identifi-

cation. Don't be surprised if you are asked to place a copy of your pass-
port, social security card, or other state or national ID on file.

✔ **Obtain (or Apply for) Keys, Security Badge, and Uniform (if needed).**
- Make sure to get a temporary badge if your permanent one will take some time to arrive.
- Attend any training or orientation.
- Review the employee manual and any other matter you're asked to read.
- Request business cards if they will be a part of your job.

✔ **Your Work Station—Getting Organized.**
- Clean your workspace when time allows, but do not make this a priority. If your cubicle has been empty for a long period of time, it may have become someone's storage space. Don't take it personally. Before you begin to move boxes and other clutter to the dumpster, enlist the help of your supervisor to give you a little direction (and any cleaning supplies). It may be there for a reason. If it looks like it will be awhile before you are able to touch base with your boss, neatly stack the stuff in a corner and don't get flustered.
- Disinfect your desk top and drawers with damp paper towels and a spray cleaner. Remember to do the same thing with everything in your cube, including your computer screen, keyboard, mouse, and mouse pad. Wipe down your chair, armrests, telephone, doorknobs, and any other place that gets handled frequently.
- Document and then request any supplies or equipment you will need.

✔ **Maximize Your Efficiency.** Now is the time to rearrange the furniture to make the layout as user friendly to you as possible. If you want your computer screen facing toward the aisle, so people who come into your cube don't startle you, now is the time to have Information Technology (IT) make the change. Do you use your telephone frequently? Put it within easy reach. Make sure your chair is adjusted to fit you comfortably. Ask for any other special adjustments or accommodations you need.

✔ **Get your Computer, Accounts, and Passwords Set Up.** The IT or IS department will usually provide help in setting up your workstation. Listen to the instructions and advice. Do not forget to ask for assistance installing a printer, if you need to.

✔ **Voice Mail System.** Activate your mailbox, record an outgoing message, and set a password.

EVERY DAY

✔ **Start Each Day with a Clean Slate.** During the first week, you may not be overwhelmed with work, but it is important to clean your desk each night. Walking into a workspace with a desk suffering from "hangover" and an overstuffed inbox can quickly lead to more stress than you probably already feel.

✔ **Organize Your Day.** Avoid getting distracted by low-priority items, such as diving into emails, when more important issues may need your immediate attention. Update your to-do list frequently and address issue number one until it is completed. Work through your top five issues. Try not to get distracted, and maximize the impact of your day by focusing on achieving results. If your boss has a critical need, reorder your priorities in favor of those issues of greatest importance.

✔ **Listen to Your Voice Mail.** You would be surprised at how many people forget to listen to voicemails. Instead, they immediately log on to their computers. Sometimes people (like your boss) may leave voice messages after work. If you forget to check, you could miss something essential.

✔ **Important Calls and Urgent Emails.** If you are on a deadline or need information the same day, make calls or send urgent emails as early as possible. If you wait until later in the day, you may not get the needed response until tomorrow or the person you need to connect with may not be available—or even in the office.

✔ **Determine Your Most Productive Time Span.** Once you have determined your peak work time, block this time out on your calendar. This reserved "do-not-disturb" time guarantees your peak time is maximized each day.

End of Every Day

The end of the day is the best time to handle paperwork and tasks that don't require phone contact, such as reports, emails, memos, and other projects requiring concentrated thought with little interruption.

✔ **Review Your Schedule for the Next Day.** Always make sure you're aware of any meetings or calls scheduled for the following day. You can use this opportunity to block out time on your calendar to accomplish any unfinished items from today's to-do list.

✔ Prioritize what you must accomplish the next day and plan how you will manage those items.. You'll probably update or add to your to-do list the following morning, but it doesn't hurt to compile a preliminary list the night before.

✔ **Clean Out Your Email Inbox.** As the end of the day nears, go through your email inbox. Now is the time to get rid of unnecessary copies, invitations, and random requests. Control your emails before they control you, ensuring that you remain on top of them, instead of getting backed up.

✔ **Don't Put Off Tomorrow What You Can Do Today.** End your workday in peace by eliminating tasks you can do quickly. Write that memo you've been putting off, answer the email from a grumpy customer, or touch base with the team member you have been meaning to see. These tasks are easy to do, so avoid putting them on the "back burner."

✔ **Before You Leave, Say Good Night.** This is a great way to end the day and remain visual to fellow team members and your boss. You can also use this time to reconfirm deadlines and receive any updates you may need to start your day tomorrow.

YOUR FIRST WEEK

✔ **Understand Your Role and How You Will Be Evaluated.** Sometimes, the responsibilities of the job as originally described to you change even before you start work. Touch base with your manager to find out what (if anything) has changed. Make sure that you have a clear understanding of your current role, responsibilities, and authority before you take on any projects.

During your conversation, create a concise and realistic ninety-day achievement plan. Then, be proactive about following up at the end of your first thirty, sixty, and ninety days to review and gauge your success.

Be sure you understand how your performance will be evaluated. Know what criteria you will be judged against to determine if you are successful. When it comes time for your performance appraisal, you don't want any surprises. Don't be afraid to ask your manager to define the requirements for success in the job.

✔ **Learn to Work with Your Boss.** Jennifer King, in *6 Things New Hires Should Do in the First 30 Days,* suggests the key to being a successful new employee is helping your boss be successful. Find out what keeps your boss up at night and come up with creative ways to alleviate those worries. Moreover, establish a positive working relationship with your manager. Find out how he or she wants to communicate with you. For example, does your manager want to meet in person every week for project updates or would he or she prefer to receive updates less frequently by email? Also, ask your boss about goals and objectives for the team. Determine how you can use your skills to help the team accomplish those goals.[1]

✔ **Craft Your Elevator Pitch.** Before you start introducing yourself to everyone, figure out what you're going to say when you meet them. Prepare concise answers for questions you will probably be asked, including:

- Your new position
- Whom you will be working for
- What you were be doing for the company
- The company or school you're coming from
- Some of your professional qualifications

Give the people you meet a reason to continue building a relationship with you.

✔ **Reach Out to Others.** Extend your hand and say your first and last name to everyone who crosses your path. Stand up straight, make direct eye contact, and remember to always smile. You may not remember the names all of the people you meet the first week on the job, but they will remember you as friendly, outgoing, and confident.

You have less than ten seconds to make an impression. A smile says "confidence" and identifies you as both approachable and friendly. Don't give others the opportunity to label you as arrogant, preoccupied, spaced out, or any other negative because of what they read into your facial expression. You'll be amazed at the effect a smile has on others.

✔ **Ask Igniter Questions.** Ask questions so that the other person can talk about himself or herself. Ask generic, business-related questions, such as:
  • What is your title?
  • What department do you work in?
  • Whom do you work for?
  • How long have you worked for the company?

Maintain eye contact and nod your head or interject comments like, "That's interesting," Ask questions that allow your associate to talk easily. "So you love to go hang gliding. What made you get into that in the first place?"

✔ **Listen Actively.** A conversation will go nowhere if you are too busy thinking of other things, including what you plan to say next. If you listen carefully, you'll identify questions to ask based on the other person's statements.

✔ **Know When the Conversation Is Finished.** Watch other people's body language. If they begin to look nervous or start to glance at their watch, the conversation is over. Smile, let them know how much you enjoyed meeting them, and say goodbye. Being concise and sensitive to their time restraints while ending on a positive note will make the other person want to talk with you again.

✔ **Take Notes.** It is unrealistic to expect to remember everything the first week of your job. Take the time to jot down the names of the people you meet and any quick comment or observation about each one. Ask for their business cards, too, which will give you the correct spelling of their names, titles email addresses, and direct dial numbers.

✔ **Learn the Business Quickly.** When receiving assignments or information from your boss, take detailed notes. Be sure to paraphrase what you heard once you've written it down. *"So you want me to create a spreadsheet showing sales by month and year for the past five years. Is that correct?"* This shows respect for the other person and gives him or her the chance to correct your understanding or affirm it, and then ensure that you produce the result that your boss is looking for.

After hearing advice from coworkers, write that down too. Here are a few things to find out:

- How formal/informal is the business environment?
- What is the true chain of command?
- How strict is management on various issues?

Don't get too comfortable too fast. Remember, you are being watched and evaluated, so follow the rules. If your boss tells you lunch breaks are 45 minutes and your coworkers tell you they take an hour and no one cares, be back at your desk in 45 minutes.

At the end of each day, get into the habit of referring to your notes and reviewing the names of those you have met during your first weeks. An added benefit is that you will connect quicker, acclimate quicker, and feel more confident and comfortable quicker.

CHECKLIST

Chapter 24—Prepared and Ready to Go

_____ Do you know when, where, and whom to meet on your first day?
_____ Have you taken care of all necessary paperwork?
_____ Have you contacted IT to set up your computer and workstation?

At the start of every day, ask:

_____   Have you arrived early enough to answer voice mail and emails?

_____   Is your desk organized and ready for a productive day?

_____   Are you continuing to introduce yourself to the office staff?

_____   Are you up and running—and learning the business quickly?

_____   If not, have you asked for help or direction?

_____   Are you learning the new culture by listening and observing?

_____   Have you remembered (and followed) your business etiquette?

25

Your First Six Months

Your First Month

✔ **Look before You Leap.** As you look around, you begin to see areas big and small that are ripe for improvement. But hold your fire and bite your tongue! It is too soon for you to offer your opinion. Move slowly, and proceed with extreme caution as you begin to navigate the new terrain of your job and company culture.

Be willing to make suggestions, but be careful not to come in guns blazing, pointing out all the different things that are broken within your department. You want your team to ask, 'What would we have done without you?" without your sending that message. Overeagerness to appear proactive can backfire. As a new hire, you won't have the historical context about why a policy or process may or may not need fixing. Or you might be suggesting "new" ideas that have already been tested. Ask questions to understand existing policies and processes. Then, you can be more effective.

Research has found that strangers who make (possibly sensible) suggestions too soon risk annoying members of the established group. This is especially true if your wonderfully, perceptive suggestions seem to suggest some kind of inherent criticism of the existing "way things are done here."[1]

✔ **Observe Meeting Etiquette.** Nancy R. Mitchell, *The Etiquette Advocate*, recommends "insuring that your meetings manners measure up"[2]:
  - Arrive on time,
  - Stand behind a chair until someone indicates where you should sit,

- Introduce yourself to others as they arrive,
- Don't arrive with a beverage in hand and place it on a meeting table until you know this is permitted and that others do so.
- Don't place your Tablet or SmartPhone on the table.
- Don't answer a call or send text messages during a meeting.
- Pay attention and be an active listener.
- Clean up your place at the table before leaving.
- Offer to help others with removing meeting materials or equipment from the room.
- If you must arrive late or leave early, inform the meeting host in advance.

✔ **Be a Good Corporate Citizen.** There is nothing more aggravating than running into the copy room to make a quick copy and finding the copier out of paper or jammed. Do your part to keep common areas stocked with supplies. If you don't know how to use the copier, ask. Don't leave your doggie bag in the refrigerator for weeks at a time. Clean up after yourself. Think about how your behavior affects others.

✔ **Do Not Burst into Another Person's Workspace.** Instead, pause. Then lightly tap before entering. Try to establish eye contact with the person before moving into the workspace. Watch the person's body language. Being new to the company, you have no idea who this person may be meeting with. If the person doesn't establish eye contact with you quickly, come back.

✔ **Knock When You Enter an Occupied Office or Conference Room.** It is extremely rude not to do so. Ask the occupant if it is an appropriate time to ask a question, share some requested information, or retrieve something. Be careful. If not invited in, do not disturb.

✔ **Observe How Others Interact with You.** Make certain your intuition is working as you begin to interact with coworkers, supervisors, managers, and officers. Each person has a unique way of dealing with people. The quicker you can identify and adapt to the style of the person, the sooner you will build a positive and productive relationship. Nancy R. Mitchell (*The Etiquette Advocate*) further comments: "Some people want only the facts and business-related data. They don't want to be your best friend and they don't want you to waste their time. Others want to hear about your weekend, family, or new apartment before starting a business discussion. Learn to read the signals that others send and adapt your approach accordingly."[3]

Your First Six Months

✔ **Learn the Overall Business.** Request a series of short informational meetings with key company players. Ask for a brief tour of their departments, and see if there are other key players you could meet as a part of these tours. Follow up with those you meet at a later date to learn more about each department.

✔ **Be Proactive About Your Ongoing "New-Hire" Orientation.** In the bustle of corporate life, you may only receive one day of orientation. Or, you may get a few days to work with the person you are replacing or even attend a couple of the regular meetings with that person. However, after that, you may be expected to stand on your own. If so, be proactive with your managers about their training plans and what you need to accomplish in your first three months on the job.

✔ **Setup a Monthly Session with Your Boss.** It is important to communicate on a regular basis in person with your boss. Create a standard format to follow. Review your ninety-day plan and discuss things like your current projects, upcoming training, unresolved issues, responsibilities, and any other procedural questions. I always found it helpful to ask if I was providing too much information, not enough, or just the right amount. From there, I would adjust the information flow. Constantly observe the personality and work style of your new manager, both in one-on-one situations and in meetings. Remember that your job is to meet the needs of your boss. It is important to always listen 80 percent of the time and talk 20 percent of the time.[4]

✔ **Alignment with Your Boss.** Always know your boss's priorities. He or she is the person who decides what's important and what's not. Here are a few things to remember:
  • Many times in stressful situations, you may not get clear direction. Use your one-on-one meeting time to clarify important tasks. Don't

be afraid to ask questions, brainstorm, and come to an agreement. Be sure to point out the trade-offs if you have to reprioritize.

- If you want to discuss a noncritical project, bring it up at the end of the meeting after you have provided updates on everything else. That way, if your meeting gets canceled, delayed, or interrupted, you will stay on track on the key issues in their order of importance as viewed by your boss.
- Eric Shannon, www.justjobs.com, recommends: "Saying 'no' to low priority items when they degrade your performance on important projects. Just as it's tempting for you to take on every project your boss mentions, it's also tempting for your boss to give you too many projects. We all have eyes that are too big for our stomachs. When you say no, you are simply introducing some reality into the discussion and that's a mark of maturity.

  You'd be wise to say 'no' gently, however. You might say something like "Eric, can you help me prioritize that in relation to my other projects?" and follow up with "based on those priorities, I'll probably be hitting that project next quarter, does that work for you?

When you focus consistently on your boss's priorities, you'll earn a reputation for strong execution, accepting guidance well, and good teamwork. Your boss will know that you understand the meaning of 'less is more.'"[5]

✔ **Overdeliver on your First Three Assignments.** Because you are new to the organization and your boss does not know you yet, overcommunicate your progress to your boss as you work through each assignment. Don't be afraid to ask questions, but be sure to bring recommendations to show how you thought about the problem. Ask for and accept feedback constructively with a smile.

✔ **Pay Attention to Company Culture.** You can always learn something about the company's culture if you watch. This is especially apparent during times of change. Some aspects of the company culture can vary from division to division. Watch how others act and you'll absorb a load of information about cultural expectations, including:

- Are people always 10 minutes early for meetings?

- Do they eat outside of the building or grab and go, eating at their desks?
- Is working on Saturday an unwritten requirement?
- What hours do most people work?
- Is there a lot of laughter and over-the-cube discussion, or do people stay silent and focused on their work?
- Do people communicate primarily through in-person meetings or by email?

Even if corporate conformity isn't your thing, following the unwritten rules stitched into the corporate culture helps you to blend in, meet expectations, and put people at ease.

✔ **Don't Turn Down Help.** Even if you don't need the help, accept assistance anyway. At a minimum, you'll begin forming bonds, but you'll also probably gain helpful information. After all, how do you know what you don't know?

✔ **Where Is the Power?** Just because a person's job description details what they are supposed to do doesn't mean they really do it. What is said on paper is often different from what really happens. Your goal is to learn how the work really gets done, and by whom.

Sam Grobart, *Money Magazine*, recommends "starting to figure out which people seem to be plugged in. Then approach them with simple questions about process ('How does Ms. Jones like to be kept informed about Project XYZ?'), steering clear of questions about personalities ('What's Ms. Jones really like?').

Chances are good that knowledgeable coworkers will pepper their responses with both types of info ('Send updates by email, and keep them short. Jones is a real cut-to-the-chase type'). This way you get the information you need without looking like you were angling for it.[6]

Corporate Buzz

Always be on the lookout for influential people within the organization. They are usually the ones whose opinions other people quote. Find a reason to work with them. Establish rapport with them (by being knowledgeable and professional), and you may suddenly "find that a whole lot more people have started to warm to your presence." When they begin to say good things about you, your value within the organization grows.

Another way to find influential people is to ask someone you have just met, "Whom else do you think I should speak to now and get to know?" You'll know you've hit a "go-to" person when several new coworkers answer with the same name, and say, "Oh, you have to speak with. . . . !"

✔ **Go the Extra Mile.** Demonstrate your preparedness to go the extra mile and be part of the business family. When extra time is required on an important project, a coworker needs help, or other special needs arise, do your part. Show you are willing to do some of the heavy lifting even if it isn't in your job description.

✔ **Last Words of Advice.** By this time, you will have developed a strong vision of your role within the company. Your level of confidence is likely to have grown significantly since your first day, and your leadership qualities have begun to become evident. Here are additional considerations:

- Now is the time to begin to recommend (or implement) those changes you've wanted to make, but start slowly.
- After six months, it is appropriate to consider expanding your presence within the company by joining committees or cross-functional teams.
- In the community, consider sitting on a not-for-profit board or join a service club.
- Take time to notice your growth, and reward yourself for your progress.

Perhaps the most important piece of advice for your first ninety-days is to establish yourself as a team player by doing more listening than speaking, said Deirdre McEachern, a certified career coach at VIPCoaching. "Too many new employees fall into the trap of trying to prove their worth by offering unsolicited opinions or making odious comparisons to 'how we did it at my last job.' Employers and fellow employees want to know you are on their team now and that you are 100 percent committed. The best way to prove your worth is to be a focused listener to your teammates around you."[7]

CHECKLIST

Chapter 25—Your First Six Months

_____ Are you continuing to expand your new-hire orientation?
_____ Have you established periodic checkpoints with your boss?
_____ Are you absorbing the business culture?
_____ Are you picking up on the power brokers of the company?
_____ Are you making your presence known as part of the team? Within the company?
_____ In the community?
_____ Are you enjoying your job and building your future?

Thank you for investing the time to read *The Job Search Checklist*. Losing your job is one of the most traumatic things that will happen to you in your life. Together we have discussed a 7-Step Process leading to reemployment, as well as the long, emotional journey you have traveled or will travel as a result of losing your job, including:

- The extremely stressful "living-in-limbo" period before a layoff or downsizing. With any luck, you had the time to decode and react to the signs of an impending layoff and prepare in advance.
- *The Emotional Impact of Job Loss (Step 1)* For me, this was the most difficult part of dealing with unemployment. I am hopeful you found beneficial tools, strategies, and advice to help deal with your personal job loss and the grieving period you and your family will survive.
- *Life After Unemployment (Step 2)* As members of Professionals in Transition® (www.jobsearching.org) have shared with me since 1992, you have probably found recovery from job loss through small daily steps. You gradually get used to it, but you never completely get over it.
- *Developing a Career Plan (Step 3)* Virtually everyone I have worked with in developing a career plan has told me that they will never get caught "flatfooted" again, which means they plan on staying in control of their careers and never getting complacent again. I encourage you to do the same.
- *Crafting an Effective Résumé (Step 4)* Now that you have created an effective platform to market and promote yourself, update your résumé at least once a year.
- *The Power of Networking (Step 5)* The single most important life skill you have learned while job searching should be networking. It will serve you well now that you are back at work.

- *Effective Interviewing (Step 6)* Successful interviewing is what landed you your next job. Although it was stressful, you nailed it! In addition, you were able to master the skillful art of how and when to effectively negotiate salary.
- *Hit the Ground Running (Step 7)* Congratulations! Enjoy the beginning of your new professional life.

Please let me know how you are doing, how this book has helped you. Send comments or suggestions to birkeldamian@gmail.com
Thank you and continued Good Luck!!!

ENDNOTES

Chapter 1: Job Loss Grieving

1. Posttraumatic stress disorder—causes, DSM, effects, therapy, adults, drug, person, people; http://www.minddisorders.com/Ob-Ps/Post-traumatic-stress -disorder.html#ixzz20H9BV200
2. http://www.helpguide.org/mental/post_traumatic_stress_disorder_syptoms _treatment.htm
3. http://www.forward.com/articles/138561/unemployment-is-an-ongoing -traumatic-stress-disord/#ixzz1rf8jKgjK

Chapter 2: Secondhand Job Loss

1. http://www.ncforeclosurehelp.org

Chapter 3: Recovery

1. http://employment.findlaw.com/losing-a-job/your-rights-when-losing-or -leaving-a-job.html
2. http://www.allbusiness.com/human-resources/workforce-management -termination
3. http://workforcesecurity.doleta.gov/unemploy/uifactsheet.asp
4. http://www.servicelocator.org/AboutThisData.asp; http://www.careeronestop .org/ReEmployment/COS_FindOneStopCenter.aspx?zip=&city=&state=AL &proximity=25&search=Search&ES=Y&EST=Find+a+location

Chapter 4: Getting Organized

1. http://blog.simplyhired.com/2010/12/get-organized-for-2011-job-search -success.html#ixzz21Bjobg1p

Chapter 5: Rebuilding Your Professional Identity

1. http://www.nightingale.com/Auth_Bio~author~Earl_Nightingale.aspx
2. http://www.biankalegrand.com/job/2010/01/is-it-only-a-job-loss-or-a-loss
   -of-selfidentity-as-well.html
3. http://www.careerjournaleurope.com/jobhunting/jobloss/19990225-gordon
   .html
4. http://community.seattletimes.nwsource.com/archive/?date=20020727&slug
   =haldane27m

Chapter 7: All-Important Research

1. http://www.npr.org/2011/02/08/133474431/a-successful-job-search-its-all
   -about-networking
2. http://articles.businessinsider.com/2012-03-08/tech/31135231_1_websites
   -domain-internet

Chapter 8: Personality Testing

1. http://www.msnbc.msn.com/id/44120975/ns/business-careers/t/employers
   -turn-tests-weed-out-job-seekers
2. http://www.msnbc.msn.com/id/44120975/ns/business-careers/t/employers
   -turn-tests-weed-out-job-seekers
3. https://cdn.theladders.net/static/images/editorial/weekly/pdfs/personality
   -job-search.pdf
4. http://www.ipat.com/16pf
5. http://www.onlinediscprofile.com/?gclid=CKGcofbk9rECFUuc7QoddTU
   AKQ
6. http://www.onlinediscprofile.com/?gclid=CKGcofbk9rECFUuc7QoddTU
   AKQ
7. http://www.myersbriggs.org/
8. https://www.cpp.com/Products/strong/strong_info.aspx
9. https://www.cpp.com/Products/firo-b/firob_info.aspx
10. https://cdn.theladders.net/static/images/editorial/weekly/pdfs/personality
    -job-search.pdf

Chapter 9: Personal Marketing Plan

1. www.careerpotential.com/articles/target-company-list-builds-focus-and-
   productivity.html

Chapter 12: Keywords: The Hidden Language of the Internet

1. www.about.com/od/jobsearchglossary/g/applicant-tracking-systems.htm
2. http://www.langpop.com/or).
3. http://theundercoverrecruiter.com/top-5-job-search-aggregators-smarter-job-hunt/

Chapter 17: Social Networking

1. http://www.pcmag.com/encyclopedia_term/0,2542,t=social%2Bnetworking&i=55316,00.asp
2. http://www.forbes.com/sites/reneesylvestrewilliams/2012/05/31/how-recruiters-use-linkedin/
3. http://theundercoverrecruiter.com/top-5-job-search-aggregators-smarter-job-hunt/
4. http://gigaom.com/2009/07/29/collaboration-with-skype-desktop-sharing-the-best-free-method/
5. http://jobsearch.about.com/od/careermanagement/a/manage.htm
6. http://www.citytowninfo.com/career-and-education-news/articles/users-dislike-new-facebook-job-search-app-12111901
7. http://www.wired.com/gadgetlab/2012/11/facebook-steps-into-professional-networking-launches-job-listing-app/
8. http://abcnews.go.com/Technology/facebook-passwords-employers-schools-demand-access-facebook-senators/story?id=16005565#.UKPdm-Oe9dI
9. http://abcnews.go.com/Technology/facebook-passwords-employers-schools-demand-access-facebook-senators/story?id=16005565#.UKPdm-Oe9dI
10. http://www.examiner.com/article/millennial-branding-and-beyond-com-release-study-on-multi-generational-job-searc
11. http://www.google.com/#hl=en&sugexp=les%3B&gs_nf=3&pq=what%20is%20skype&cp=10&gs_id=j&xhr=t&q=what+is+voip&pf=p&sclient=psyab&oq=what+isvoi&gs_l=&pbx=1&bav=on.2,or.r_gc.r_pw.r_qf.&fp=47a2fcfaf4647c4e&bpcl=35466521&biw=1067&bih=402
12. http://jobsearch.about.com/od/careertests/a/careertests.htm
13. http://jobsearch.about.com/od/jobinterviewtypes/qt/situational-interview.htm
14. http://jobsearch.about.com/od/behavorialinterviews/a/behavioral-interview-questions.htm
15. http://www.yorku.ca/fes/careers/jobsearch/interview.htm
16. http://candocareer.com/job-interview-questions/non-directive.htm

Chapter 22: Strategies to Ace an Interview

1. http://jobsearch.about.com/od/interviewsnetworking/a/dressforsuccess.htm
2. http://www.careerbuilder.com/Article/CB-746-Getting-Hired-The-Interview-Body-Language-Dos-and-Donts/
3. http://www.openlearningworld.com/books/Gestures%20and%20Expressions/Gestures%20and%20Expressions/Positive%20Gestures.html
4. http://www.peaseinternational.com/shopcontent.asp?type=topfives
5. http://www.careerbuilder.com/Article/CB-746-Getting-Hired-The-Interview-Body-Language-Dos-and-Donts/
6. http://www.peaseinternational.com/shopcontent.asp?type=topfives

Chapter 23: The Salary Negotiation Process

1. http://online.wsj.com/article/SB124977651986217193.html
2. http://lifeislikethat.hubpages.com/hub/How-Human-Capital-and-Human-Resources-are-different)
3. http://jobsearch.about.com/od/job-offers/a/joboffer.htm

Chapter 24: Prepared and Ready to Go

1. http://blog.softwareadvice.com/articles/hr/new-hire-checklist-1071312/

Chapter 25: Your First Sixth Months

1. http://www.uncommonhelp.me/articles/stressed-about-starting-your-new-job
2. http://www.experience.com/alumnus/article?channel_id=career_management&source_page=oh_behave&article_id=article_1210283358282
3. http://www.experience.com/alumnus/article?channel_id=career_management&source_page=oh_behave&article_id=article_1210283358282
4. http://academy.justjobs.com/the-complete-career-guide-to-working-smart/
5. http://academy.justjobs.com/live-by-your-bosss-priorities/
6. http://money.cnn.com/2006/12/27/magazines/moneymag/newguy.moneymag/index.htm
7. http://www.theladders.com/career-advice/build-relationships-early-for-job-success

INDEX